ON THE OUTSIDE
This, That & Everything in Between

by Bobby Collins

For more information contact at:
ISBN Print: 978-0-9994314-1-2

Library of Congress Control Number: Pending

Have Bobby perform at your organization or special event
contact bobbycollins.com

Layout and design: **Steven Adler**
Editor: **Sally Lentz**
Graphic Design: **Lauren Driscoll**
Illustrator: **Susan Lavalley Weaver**
Publishing Consultant: **Steven Adler WoW! Publishing and Distribution**
Printed in the United States of America

INTRODUCTION

●

YESTERDAY IS HISTORY. TOMORROW IS A MYSTERY. TODAY IS A GIFT.
THAT'S WHY IT IS CALLED THE PRESENT.
-Alice Morse Earle

I'm sitting for the second time in my life to write another book. In case you missed it, my first book was: *ON THE INSIDE, Witisims and Wisdomisms.* It was the result of my wife basically telling me to put up (actually write down) things for my daughter or shut up. Things my wife called, "Silly sayings." Regardless of what they're called, the book contained important life lessons that I wished someone had shared with me. The response I received from that book has been overwhelming! For that I am grateful. Learning that the stories I shared and lessons I wrote about, in some small way, touched people's lives was humbling. Thank you.

That was then. The world in which I wrote that book...no longer exists. Hello Covid-19! To be sure, time will forever be referred to as - pre and post covid. While people worldwide are now being vaccinated, realistically I feel, this pandemic (and it's life altering aftermath) is far from over. The underbelly of this country, and the world, has been exposed. From social unrest, economic downturn, and systemic racism. Oh, and let's not forget, lack of National leadership...I'm just waiting for that Armageddon Asteroid! During this time of isolation and quarantine, I (along with everyone else) have spent a lot of time reflecting on who I am... who we are as a country. I feel the reset button has been pushed, and now it's up to each of us to face some hard realities and make some smarter choices. We have the opportunity to take a critical look at what we want to project to others. Up to this point, a lot of people have been able to mask some ugly truths. The unaccountability, prejudices, greed and inequality... this is not God's picture for humanity! We have this moment in time to better ourselves, our relationships, and this great nation.

I have to be honest, the anxiety of not working for these months on end has been draining. At the same time, it has me thinking about how I can make some (suggested) improvements on myself. Being confined for months with loved ones will do that! At the same time so much of what

3

has defined this past year, we have had zero control over. What has gone on in the world outside, has never affected so many. Which is why I've written this second book. In it I will share some observations about stress, anger, sadness, laughter, anxiety, boredom, worry and love.

ON THE OUTSIDE, This, That and Everything In Between, is the title I chose because, I cover family, money, and some of my own insecurities...

in short...this, that and everything in between! Just as in the first book, I try to set an example for my children. To illustrate what it takes to keep your heart in the right place through thick and thin (even in today's discord) and the importance of sharing our laughter!

As I told my daughter, "Now more than ever...It's Grow up Time." So, let's put on those Big Boy/Girl Panties (I'm wearing mine right now) as we work together to rebuild our world, to ensure the "Outside" is kind, caring, and fair...for everyone!

Chapter 1

WHAT I'VE LEARNED AS A ROADS SCHOLAR

●

LIFE IS 10 PERCENT WHAT YOU MAKE IT,
AND 90 PERCENT HOW YOU TAKE IT.

-Irving Berlin

Sometime in my early stand-up days, just as I was coming off the stage at New York's comedy club, *Catch a Rising Star*, a man says, as he hands me his card, "Have your agent get in touch with me." I came back at him with, "You mean my parents?" I didn't have an agent. I have known many agents and worked with a few through the years, and to me it's like this. Have you ever seen a nature documentary about Hippos? The hippos are surrounded by schools of barbell fish, whose very existence depends on them first attaching themselves and then sucking the skin of the hippo. The trick is not to let them suck down to the bone!

However, I did know a guy who was with the ICM Agency, a first-class talent agency. I liked him okay enough. So, I called him about the guy who gave me his card. "How do you know this guy?", he asked me. "He gave me his card the other night after a set at Catch," I answered. There was a pause. "Bobby, this guy is a huge manager, he reps stars like Cher!" That did it. I signed with ICM and I now have an agent. Not long after that he called me, "Pack up, you're going to Minnesota...You're opening for (wait for it) Cher."

The first concert with Cher was an outdoor venue outside of...I have no idea what city, Lake Something or Happy Wherever. Anyway, it was a festival culminating in a Cher concert. I arrived before Cher, there were people spread out all over. People were swimming, eating and having a great time. As the time for Cher to perform got closer the crowd began centralizing and settling down. That's when I realized just how HUGE this place was. There must have been something like thirty thousand people! All I could see were bodies sitting shoulder to shoulder, filling up the landscape. Some were even hanging from trees.

Here's a widely known secret. Cher is notoriously afraid of flying. Her stateside mode of transportation? Bus. When the time to start the concert arrived...Cher's bus had not. I would be almost another 2 hours before her bus turned in the lot. A fact that did not sit well with this crowd. Finally, an announcement was made. "CHER HAS ARRIVED!" The crowd went nuts. I was told to get ready. I got ready and waited and waited. (If you've ever been to a Cher concert then you know...she doesn't just put on a costume. She IS the costume!)

What started as a soothing chant quickly grew into shouting, "CHER, CHER, CHER!" I was told, "Do a twenty-to-thirty-minute warm-up then get off." A faceless voice boomed, "Now go!" With that, I stepped out onto the stage to an enthusiastic, "Please welcome comedian Bobby Collins!" In case you are wondering...thousands of people booing you is most definitely NOT a confidence booster! I had never worked in front of this many people...ever. All I knew was performing in comedy clubs around the New York, New Jersey area. Now I'm standing before a massive crowd, who are loudly letting me know, they do not want to listen to some schmuck telling jokes. I couldn't blame them. They had waited hours for their idol. These were loyal, dedicated fans, of course they were disappointed and upset. But I had a job to do. Did I panic? Absolutely...on the inside. Did I freeze up? I did not. I did however set the world's record for the worst "Flop Sweat." The faucets in my armpits opened wide up. Sweat was gushing directly down into my underwear! I was sure the people closest to the stage could hear me sloshing as I paced around.

Then something magical happened. After about five minutes, I'd made friends with them. By the end of my set not only were they laughing, they were cheering and clapping. The lesson here? Learn to read the room QUICKLY! Then adjust. Get comfortable every time you go on stage, everywhere you perform.

When I came off stage the man in charge says, "Good job" before he moved quickly to get Cher on stage. I stood on the side of the stage and watched her awesome performance, then went to change (don't forget that flop sweat - I never have.)

I learned a lot from opening for Cher. Before each show she would have singers, dancers, lighting and sound crews, everyone backstage, hold hands and offer up a prayer for a great show. I especially loved the way she made it a point to have the people in wheelchairs taken to the front row, the best seats, right in front of the stage. This happened at every venue... every show. Having a special needs child, this thoughtful act meant a great deal to me.

Watching her performances, I learned how to be comfortable on a large stage. It is different from the smaller, intimate space of comedy clubs. I learned how to utilize the space effectively. To move around and keep the audience involved. I saw how important it is to look up and speak as you would person to person. These were valuable lessons, indeed.

I also learned I am definitely NOT a "Jump on the bus, Gus" guy. Because I was in the opening act, I got the back of the bus. The hum of the highway never let me get a full night's sleep. I'd wake up in the middle of the night and go sit up with the driver. This cowboy hat wearing "Good Ol' Boy" would have his fingers vigorously tapping away on the steering wheel while some country western tune was blasting away. He was totally impervious to the size and weight of the vehicle that he was barreling through the night. Not to mention the fact there were living bodies packed away for the night...directly behind him! I remember one night, as he was pulling out of a hair-raising curve, he let out a loud, whooping, "Heee Hawww!" As I was wiping terrified tears from my eyes, I just as loudly, caterwauled, "We're all going to die!" Nope never again. From then on, it's been "Fly the Friendly Skies" for me.

Our next tour stop was Long Island's Jones Beach Theater, also an outside venue. Coming home to New York is always special, there would be no flop sweat here. I was gaining confidence and further developing my ability to "read the room." The key to this, I also learned, is simple. You must GO ON THE ROAD. You learn people react to material in different parts of the country (sometimes in different parts of the same city). This means you have to leave your hotel room (or bus)! Pay attention on the drive to the venue. Is it in the heart of a large city, or out in a suburb? Once there, take a few minutes and actually walk around, even if it's only for a couple of blocks. Are the streets lined with Mercedes' or pick-up trucks? What businesses do you see? Listen in on conversations. Are the locals talking about the stock market? Or how their kid just won a blue ribbon at the county fair. Are they discussing the latest book they're reading? Or lamenting about their shift at the plant getting cut. Trust me, all this observation and eavesdropping will help you understand the intelligence, worries, and joys of this room full of strangers...your audience. You will learn to Read The Room! Ah, but then you have to apply what you've observed and heard in order to utilize these differences by adapting your material according.

I have also found people are more likely to entertain tough subject matters or accept a different point of view when it's packaged in laughter. Your first duty to your audience is to get them to laugh. However, keep in mind you also have a responsibility to educate. No audience is comfortable being preached at. Just present your material so that it gets (and keeps) them laughing. If you've provided some new insights...all the better! Hold up that mirror, send them home with a smile and the understanding that we're all in this together and you've got yourself a Win Win!

During the Cher tour, I was asked to perform as an emergency opener for Ol' Blue Eyes himself...Frank Sinatra. His opening act, Tom Dressen had gotten sick. They wanted me to fill in. I was picked up in a private plane and taken to Salt Lake City, for his first show. Just like in the movies, there's a limo waiting to rush me to the venue. I arrive and quickly change clothes. A big guy, (BIG like 6'6") named Gilly is giving me the heads up. "Don't call him Frank, It's Mister Sinatra. Only speak to him if he speaks to you first." I'm taken into the room where Mr. Sinatra is with his entourage. His people are answering phones, calling people, going over seating, and stage directions. I'm introduced to guys who all seemed to be named after body parts. There was Tony the arm, Vinnie the nose, Stevie the foot...you get the picture. Body Parts Squad was answering phones that were ringing all around the room. Frank, er Mr. Sinatra is sitting next to a silent phone. Suddenly it rings, the entire room went dead quiet. In unison, all heads turn and eyes widen as HE answers it. I could hear the voice on the phone, it was the head sound technician asking for the sub star (that would be me) to come down for a sound check. Mr. Sinatra curtly replies, "He's the opening comic, just put the power on." His steely Baby Blues are now locked on me as he asks, "You okay with that"? The wisdom of my inner New York street kid kicks in - Now is not the time to get killed for being a wise ass comic. I manage a cool, calm collected, "No problem - I'm good to go." With that, the room returns to nonstop phones ringing. Tony the arm, Larry the liver, or some member of the Body Parts Squad answers one of the phones, then calls out, "Boss, it's that old stripper from Hoboken. Ginny remember?" Frank comes back with, "Sure give her a couple of tickets."

Mr. Sinatra's shows are all sold out. I go on stage, do my job, and had fun. It helped that it was Frank Sinatra's audience because my east coast attitude fit in well with the crowd. Afterwards, I stick around to watch him from the side of the stage and to see how he works. A master, beautiful to watch. I thought it was cool that his orchestra was led by his son, Frank Sinatra Jr. In the middle of his show, I go to my dressing room to change. I thought I could go over to the local comedy club to work on some material. I ain't gonna to lie. I may have been going over in my mind, how I might just let it 'slip' that I was in town, opening for Frank Sinatra (wouldn't you?). I figured if I got to a club early, I could get back in time, to hopefully hang out with Mr. Sinatra. Before I could leave, his boy Gilly comes up and tells me, "The boss enjoyed your act. He'd like you to join him for dinner, in Chicago, along with some other people after he finishes the show". I told him my plans to hit a comedy club tonight and that I'd just fly out in the morning and meet up in Chicago tomorrow night. In a low, slow, guttural growl he repeats, "Maybe you didn't hear me. The BOSS enjoyed your show and has asked you to join him for dinner!" I managed to squeak out, "No problem, I'm getting ready right now." To be honest, I've never been into that whole Italian loyalty thing (unlike my Italian wife) or idolizing the whole Frank Sinatra "I did it my way." thing. However, the man was paying me great money, and my mother didn't raise no dummy...so it was dinner tonight in Chicago. They put me into one of the waiting limos, then with a police escort, we are off to the airport. Above all, I'm a team player.

We arrive in Chicago and are whisked away in another stretch limo to a restaurant called the Pump Room. It's about one o'clock in the morning. There are about twelve of us sitting down ordering dinner. I'm really ready to go to bed but, hey, I'm a bit player in the Godfather now! Low and behold in walks Don Rickles. He greets everyone warmly, openly fawning over Frank. He walks by me, introduces himself and informs me that Frank really liked my show. I eat, listen, learn and watch. Here it is, three o'clock in the morning and all the waiters at this closed restaurant will get tipped more than I was making to perform that night. The lesson here? Always, I mean always, treat the staff well! Something I've never forgotten.

Every entertainer has their style. After performing with many of the best Comics, I could feel my style developing. I learned that it was not just the telling of a story that brings the laugh, but letting the audience feel who you are telling the story. It is allowing people to know you and enjoy that journey from where that story is coming from and taking the audience along to share in it. That my friend is what I see missing in many of the performers coming up nowadays. Their failure to allow that personal insight into who you are. Lesson learned!

It was during this early part of my career that I lived in a small studio apartment in the Village neighborhood in Manhattan, N.Y. I decided to rent it out to move across the East River, to Cobble Hill, Brooklyn, into a seven-room brownstone with a third-floor walkup. That means no elevator. It cost the same as I was paying for that small studio. It was a twenty-minute subway ride to get back into the city. The bigger living space made it well worth the extra money and inconvenience. I joined a health club in the Heights neighborhood. The club had an extremely competitive basketball league and life was beautiful. One day after playing basketball, I went to get my car where I always parked. As I was pulling out of my space a huge limousine was blocking me from leaving the garage. I honked my horn a few times and rolled my window down and hollered "OK, asshole time to move it!" A big man resembling Odd Job from a Bond movie, gets out of the car and starts walking over to me. He's Huge. I wondered how he managed to pee. I started to roll up my window ...slowly. He walks right over to my window and says, "How about I put my cock in your mouth?" Startled, I'm quickly rolling up my window all the way now and I'm saying to myself, who says that to another human being? I smile and wave signaling – No problem, I'll wait. He turns and goes back to his car. He keeps me waiting for about fifteen minutes. He finally leaves. I pull out of the garage and go on my way. I come back the next day and the lady who runs the garage is in a rage. She stops me and tells me, "Get out of here, go away. Don't come back here and park anymore. That car yesterday? The one you honked at! That was mob boss John Gotti's car. They took down your license plate number, get out of here!" She blocks me from entering, so I leave.

I'm not a fearful person, but the next night my girlfriend, who used my car from time to time, said, "You know, I think another car was following me, from the market to our apartment. Weird right?" Why would you lead them to our doorstep! "Yeah, weird," is all I can come up with. A few days pass, I go back to the health club and park in a totally different neighborhood. After playing ball with the guys, I go up to the locker room to shower and change. A guy who I always see and have exchanged pleasantries with at the gym is getting changed in front of his locker. I say "Hi." and start to change. He says under his breath, but just loud enough for me to hear "You know you have to go over to his house and apologize." I look at him and ask, "What are you talking about?" He hands me a piece of paper and leaves. It's John Gotti's address in Brooklyn. I stare at it for a minute. What is this Good Fellas? I'm not going to do that! Then I remember what my girlfriend told me about a car following her. I thought, maybe something bad could happen to her, or to me, or both of us. I don't need to be a New York Post Headline! Later that night, I decide to go out with my friend Larry, for a night of fun. I pick him up, and as we're driving, I tell him, "We need to make a quick stop first." We go to the address that I was given at the gym, park, go up the stairs. The door opens, we step inside and we're both patted down. As we're ushered into a room, we pass groups of men hanging out talking, drinking, smoking and playing cards. We walk into a large room where the heavy hitters are hanging out with John Gotti. I recognized them from their pictures in the papers. I introduce myself, then start to apologize about the whole parking lot thing. He cuts me off, smiles and says, "No. it's all right, I hear you're a comedian and funny one at that." He introduces me to a few of the boys, then says, "Can I ask you a favor? I've got this 'function' coming up, how about you do some comedy for me that night?" I quickly fire back, "I saw the Godfather and once a favor is given a debt is owed". He cracks up laughing and then his boys start laughing. As Larry and I are about to leave to get back to my car, Larry looks at me and says quietly, "Bobby, these guys all look like they kill people." I come back with, "They probably do, let's get out of here." Larry is in the car screaming at me, "Did you know who that was, before you brought me, a nice Jewish boy, to see a mobster...at his house!"

Through the years, I've been hired to work a few times for different groups of people. What I've learned is this. "Respectable" men wearing suits and ties, who work for big corporations, can be just as bad (and sometimes worse) as men named after body parts.

I was on a roll. I received a call from my agent inquiring about opening for Dolly Parton. It was to be at Caesars Palace in Atlantic City, New Jersey, for two nights, two shows and very good money. I agree and I'm on my way to my backyard, Jersey. I get there and I'm excited. I'm introduced, come out on stage and open the show, I'm having fun. The audience is having a ball as well. I end my portion of the show and go backstage. While they're setting up the stage for Dolly to come out, I meet her. She turns to me and says, "Great show," I thank her for the opportunity, and she goes on stage. I watch some of her show from the side of the stage, smiling as I listen to familiar songs I've heard on the radio. I'm not a big Country Western fan. That hump me, dump me, let's have sex on the truck bumper, really isn't music I listen to. But, I enjoyed her professionalism and her grace. I really enjoyed watching the crowd, this was the first time she was ever playing in the Northeast. I watched most of the show and then headed back to the dressing room to change to then go out and have some fun at one or two of Atlantic City's cool spots. I receive a knock on the door and it's a woman who works for Dolly, she would like to speak to me. Of course, what's up? She says, "Well...we all enjoyed your show, but we would like you to tone it down." Always one to please, I respond, "Did a swear word slip out? Did I say something off color?" Sometimes in the moment, unintentionally, it can happen. But I didn't think so. She continued, "No, it's just that Dolly would like you to tone it down please." I read people pretty well. What she meant was, the audience loved you, but you need to remember this is Dolly's show, so you need to dial it back. You're just the opening act...Get it! Admittedly, I was a little taken aback. To me, if the opening act does very well, that helps the main act. WRONG! They don't want you to hit one out of the park. That's to be left for the Star of the show. I was quite surprised by this. Didn't matter anyway, (team player) besides, I only had one more night, before I would collect my check and head back home. The next day I arrived early and figured I'd be the bigger person. When I got there, I went to say Hi to the Nashville band guys and all her people. They were cold as ice, not at all friendly, no acknowledgement, no "Hi, great job last night," nothing. Okay, so that's how we're doing this. Bobby do the job, be professional and move on. I did the job, thanked the right people, as well as Dolly, and left. My agent called me up the very next day informing me that Dolly Parton would like me to go on a small month and a half tour with her. I tell him about the 'dressing down' I received and respond, "No thanks," I don't want to be around people who are stone cold and don't want to enjoy the experience. Not fun! Here's a roundup to all this. Dolly writes a book some eight months later and in the list of acknowledgements, one was to me. There it was, Bobby Collins among others she wanted to thank. I thought to myself, maybe she felt slighted about me not joining her on that tour and threw me an olive branch. Whatever the reason just seeing that acknowledgment - Wow. That was, as they say in country western jargon, a HOOT!

Ray Romano

Lilly Tomlin

Tom Hanks

Chapter 2

THREE TIME'S THE CHARM

●

WHEN THE SOUL IS READY, ITS MATE WILL APPEAR.
-Unknown

How can I write about my personal journeys without including the adventures of my heart? In college I was seeing the most attractive girl named Jackie, she was the most intelligent person I knew. We met up after I left Long Island, and she moved from Queens, to attend the University of Buffalo. We were young, living on our own away from home, discussing what we saw as our places in the world. Even after college, when we'd both moved back to our parents' homes, we remained a couple. She knew my best friend Alan, they had both attended the same high school, Marin Van Buren High School in Queens NY. Jackie was Valedictorian of their high school class. Alan's mother knew Jackie's parents. I remember one time after college I was visiting Alan at his mother's, when she blurted out, "Why is Jackie with you and not with my son Alan?" We both blankly stared at her, until Alan broke the awkwardness with, "Don't you just wonder what kind of party goes on in her head?"

I truly loved Jackie. She was smart, we could talk about life and discuss issues at hand, plus we laughed... a lot! She was a very straightforward person, and I loved that about her. She knew what she wanted and went after it. Her dream was, we both find satisfying careers, settle down, get married, have kids and live a life of love and happiness. I, however, was wide open to life's vast possibilities. What career do I want to pursue? Where do I want to live? What do I want out of life? She felt the stirring inside of me. However, I think she thought eventually 'I'd come around, and we would be together for the rest of our lives. As our relationship grew, I could sense her uneasiness about me and my direction. Again, follow your dreams. Even though time spent with her was glorious, I did not want to stand in her way, to eventually be the cause of her unhappiness. She had her mind set on a storybook life on Long Island. The strain was beginning to show. It was becoming evident, we had different dreams, different paths.

Every Wednesday night I'd take a ride out to CW Post College to play basketball with some really fun, mostly single guys. We would all laugh together, tell stories and enjoy each other's company. There was this one guy Brian, a smart, good looking Chiropractor. I'm not sure exactly when it happened but a thought crossed my mind, this guy would be Perfect for Jackie! Yes, it was surprising, and frankly, more than a little uncomfortable. However, I knew in my core, they would be a great fit! Yep, you guessed it, after a Wednesday night game, I introduced them. A little while later, I bowed out and let him know I was out of the picture. He stepped up and it worked. Long story short, they're married, living in Florida, children, and very happy! Here's the odd thing about this story that I don't understand. I've played in theaters near where they live in Florida and friends of theirs, who are fans of mine, attend my shows. Through the years they have told me, "You know. Jackie always loves to hear about you, your shows, how you're doing, how you look…bla bla bla"

Naturally, I ask, "So why doesn't she ever come to a show?" They confide, "Brian feels really awkward. You know, that whole you dating her first, then introducing them." Apparently, Jackie (ever the dutiful one) goes along with her husband's insecurity. Ok, as a guy, I get it. But come on… it's been forty years! See what I mean? Perfectly matched - and she's happy! With the "Almost wife" free to follow her path, I pursued my Comedy career. Out doing sets every night at different clubs all over the city. Uptown, Downtown, Long Island, and Queens; while "workin' the day job, with Calvin Klein in the Garment Center. I moved to Queens - it was halfway between Manhattan (day job) and Long Island (parents' home.) I saved my money and paid my rent. I liked being close to the grassy parks, the restaurants, and the pace of Queens. There was the availability of parking, my living space was bigger (and cheaper) than Manhattan apartments. It just felt more open for me and provided some breathing space for my head. Besides, it was only about a 20-minute drive from working night sets in the clubs to home. I felt at ease. Occasionally, I'd meet up with friends at different places, to have a meal or a drink, before heading home (early enough so I could hit my "day job," the next morning). I was that young, single, fun loving NYC guy! Wait – did I just say that?

One night I stopped in Long Island at a place called Roslyn. Beautiful quaint town, with a small pond at the center, nice restaurants and clubs. The venue was called Raffles, a fun style eatery and drink place. I walked in, looked around and saw so many young ladies hanging out, HELLO,

I'm Bobby Big Cock! On the inside (calm down, Me Too movement). I was NOT the usual guy with the loud music and drinking, screaming to be heard. I was the guy who would see someone of interest, look in them in the eye and start up a conversation. Which is what I did with this beautiful young lady Jodi. We spoke, she was sweet, caring and the type of woman who knew what she wanted and would stop at nothing to get it. Red Flag Ding Ding Ding We began dating, after a while she kept telling me, "Bobby, you have to move into the city. Manhattan is where you need to be! It's the only place you'll be successful in the world of comedy and entertainment." She went so far as to inform me of an opening in her 12th Street apartment building, at a great price. I went to look at the second floor, the largest studio apartment, I had ever seen. Plus, there was a surprise bonus...a private outdoor patio! I rented it the next day (that's the way things work in Manhattan, quick and to the point)! Unbeknownst to me – I was paying cheap rent in a (at the time) tough neighborhood. However, the location made it perfect for easily getting around town. Besides, there was Jodi, up on the seventh floor keeping an eye on me. Ding Ding Ding. She later told me, that night she saw me in Roslyn's, she announced to her friends, "That's the guy I'm going to marry."

So, there I was, living on 12th Street, making my way. Holding the day job, working the clubs, no real agenda, enjoying every day and dating this nice young lady (just an elevator ride away). Believe me... Marriage was the farthest thing from my mind! My contented life was full, writing funny material, performing comedy, paying rent, a little traveling for gigs and above all - having fun! Don't get me wrong, there were times, I'd be in some shithole hotel, performing at Joeys shithole club, missing parties, friend/family gatherings and special occasions. Of course, I would get lonesome. However, I was no cloistered monk! I'd see different ladies on the road and enjoy their company but there was never anyone serious. Then, when I'd get home Jodi would be there. We'd have "sleep-overs," hang out and have fun. Did I ever think this was the girl I would marry and start a family with – NEVER! For right now it was convenient, fun and easy! Besides, Jodi was pursuing a career in acting. Because our days were non-stop auditions, readings, acting classes, club dates, and commercials, I just assumed she was Circus People too - no time for marriage or any else for that matter.

As for comedy clubs and their rise in the late 80's – you'd leave town on a Tuesday, travel to clubs around the country and not come back until

Sunday – that was the regiment. Then when you were home your nights were at the local comedy clubs, hoping an agent or manager would see you perform and represent you! Ahh the joy of Show Business. I was moving and shaking! Playing ball with the guys Sunday mornings, doing laundry that afternoon and eating cheap Sunday night dinners. Then out of nowhere, Jodi tells me she would like to get married! We had been seeing each other for a while, enjoying our fun, busy lives, caught up in this crazy world of entertainment. Wait a minute ....all our friends from college and high school were getting married. They all were pursuing jobs, careers, dating that special someone, committing to the big M word. Could we handle a marriage with all this going on? Well, they were making it work – the pressure was on!

To marry or not to marry, that became THE topic of our discussions. I questioned whether or not we could sustain a marriage, while pursuing our dreams. Jodi assured me that we could. To her point, I was getting older, maybe it was time to be an actual adult. But, deep down I really didn't know if this is what we should be doing. I pointed out, "We are just getting up steam. Now is our time to remain focused on our end game. To support ourselves as full time, working Comedian and Equity Actress." After many animated back and forth conversations, we landed on - Ok, let's give it a shot! Breathe, Bobby breathe, maybe the subject will slip her mind. Yeah right!

I was finally home, after being on the road for two weeks straight. That first morning back, I woke up to, "While you were gone, my parents invited us over for dinner at their club in New Rochelle, New York. We're expected to meet them there tonight, at eight o'clock." Mid yawn I protested, "No way! I just got home. I'm playing ball with guys, then coming home to relax and chill out." Added to that I have never even met her parents! However, I had heard her mother is the boss with a capital B, and her father takes orders well. In this case, Jodi being the oldest, with 2 younger siblings, seems to be a student of her mother's MO. Reconsidering, I figure a great (free) dinner and maybe some fun with her family wasn't that much of a sacrifice on my part. We arrive at the club, and are shown to the table, where her entire family is already seated, with serving bowls of food placed around the table. You can cut the tension with a knife! I can tell her brother and sister were really nice kids, despite being under the sword of their mother. Jodi's father? I wanted to pull the table leg out of his ass and assure him everything will be Okay. As we sit down, I'm introduced to everyone. Jodi, trying to lighten the mood, is telling her mother about the drive from the city. I was warm and courteous while filling up my plate, hey, I was hungry. Then Old Faithful just Blew! With no lead in, her mother very loudly proclaimed, "So am I to understand you're going to marry my daughter? I don't even know who you are!" Being a fun hearted guy – I stand up, extend my hand and say, "Hi I'm Bobby Collins, the pleasure is all mine." The kids crack up, her father keeps staring down at the napkin in his lap, and her mother? Her mother is about to have an apoplectic event of major proportions! Jodi doesn't say - one - word. Ding Ding Ding I stand up and sincerely state, "I'm sorry, it was not my intention to make anyone feel uncomfortable. Jodi, I'm leaving now. You may join me or stay here with your family." Then I drove home. I felt insulted, uncomfortable and hungry. Not surprisingly, I was disappointed with Jodi, not to mention her parents. Look, I understand - your daughter shows up with some guy, who's now going to be part of your family. Naturally, there's going to be some adjustment time, but at the very least, show them some civility. My family would never have acted in such a manner! We were taught to show everyone respect and kindness, to treat them with dignity. Trust me, you'll be the one to benefit in the long run! Jodi came home later that evening to find me already writing material about the chaos at the country club, "Did you ever meet your future in-laws and wonder what planet they come from?" She apologized for her parents' behavior, and tried to assure me they'd "do better," and everything would be alright. My spidey sense was screaming...this marriage is at best...a BAD idea. But I softened, I let Jodi convince me we would still be the people we wanted to be. I convinced myself to set the example, they had gone low...I would go high. I would step up and help her realize her dreams, in spite of her abysmal family. Together we would carve out a happy, productive life together. With that, we got married.

Hold on, back up a minute. I asked a close friend of mine Paula, a Black woman whom I love dearly, to be a bridesmaid along with Jodi's friends. Well, the shit hit the fan with that. (Hello racism!) Jodi informs me, "My parents let me know they feel, there are already enough bridesmaids". Hello...who's wedding was this? My response, "Oh, Okay. Then she'll be a groomsman instead. She'll look great in a tuxedo!" She became a bridesmaid.

Now the twist to the story …. are you ready? Do you want to freshen your beverage, visit the powder room? About three months later I received a call at work from Jodi's father. He wants me to meet him for lunch. I'd rather have lunch with a woodchuck... be the bigger man Bobby, "Sure that would be nice." I have never understood, or accepted his behavior, or refusal to speak up to his wife about the whole meet and greet dinner situation. He informs me Jodi's mother has cancer. She's dying and he's not telling Jody, or the other kids. Shocked, I ask, "Why not?" He tells me he doesn't want to burden them! I tell him, "It's going to be more of a burden if you don't tell them! To be there for a loved one when a crisis arises, surrounded by your family, is a blessing." Low and behold, she goes to the garage one night, starts the car, leaves it running and dies of asphyxiation – and the young son finds her body! Her son will carry that horrible burden the rest of his life. This family was devastated, I mean they didn't know who to turn to. It was sad to see a family who relied so much on the mother to handle things, that this threw them off bigtime! Which may be a partial explanation for why the father asks me to do the eulogy for his wife! Are you kidding me? She didn't like me, and I was, at best indifferent toward her! Go big Bobby! I suppose in their minds, they thought a person who stands in a room alone, and delivers jokes, is capable of standing alone and delivering a eulogy. Whatever his reason, I chose the high road, and agreed.

I asked my good friend (the same friend, who raised racist objections for being a bridesmaid at our wedding) to help me out, and together we wrote a touching tribute to Jody's mom. As for the eulogy - everyone loved it, it was about the love of life and the joy of living and participating in each other people's lives. It was as if I were brought into this family for this specific reason – I felt it and kind of knew it to be true – Hey God, you wouldn't have given the task if I couldn't handle it, lesson learned. After such emotional turmoil with her family and seeing the price it was taking on Jodi and her siblings, I knew this was not the relationship I wanted to be in. Three months later the marriage was over. One year of marriage was my wake-up call to move on and travel with my eyes completely open. Live and learn! I moved out of my $500 a month apartment and rented it out for $550. I moved into a three story, walk up brownstone apartment, in an area called Brooklyn Heights, Brooklyn. It had seven rooms. Two bedrooms, a fireplace, living room, dining room and a television room – all for $600. It was costing me $50 to live like a king in New York City! In New York you have to learn how to work it – that comes from your street knowledge.

To this day, thirty-five years later I still have my apartment in the same building as does Jodi- me on the 2nd floor, she on the 7th floor. We're very cordial to each other. She's friendly with Jill, as well as my children. She never married to my knowledge or had a boyfriend or for that matter a girlfriend (the doormen tell me everything.) She'll be walking her dog and ask me to walk with her, I kid around and remind her, "There's a reason for that X you know." Recently as we were walking, she asked me if I remembered what I said to her when we parted and went our own ways. I did, but said I didn't. "You told me, 'If I stayed with you my head would explode!'" I laughed, she chuckled, and we moved on! Again, I feel for her and am sorry for the pain or lonesomeness she feels but life's short – make the most out of it and look at the things that make you upset, sad, angry and change them and get on with your life! There's someone out there for everyone, if that's what you want, it will come.

My present wife Jill is the girl of my dreams! Beautiful, smart, fun, giving, happy, caring, responsible, loving, supportive, funny, sexy, strong – my fingers are getting tired! I was asked in my early stage of performing to appear at this club in New Jersey above a well-known bar set up to be a performing Comedy area. A young radio DJ, by the name of Howard Stern was part owner and a Comedy manager Rick (later to be Tim Allen's and Drew Carey's manager.) I agreed, it paid pretty good and was close to the city, so I might hop back in and hit the clubs for spots! I arrive and am taken back to the green room (why do they call it the green room? It's never green - I have no idea, but it's been referred to by that name my whole career) I'm sitting laughing with Howard, and a friend or two. All of a sudden, a young waitress comes in and sits a couple of drinks down for the entertainers – her butt was right in front of me...Oh my God it was beautiful! I said, "Excuse me." She turned around and I looked into the most beautiful eyes I've ever seen. She looks at me and says, "Don't say a word, I heard you're a snake." I looked at her surprised, "Who told you that?" She pointed to Rick! I respond, "He's trying to get into your pants, I'm a straight up guy (palms up), I'm going to wine you, dine you, open the car door for you. We'll date awhile and then down the line; I'd be looking to get - you know - in... she laughed. She watched my performance, (laughed hard) and afterwards agreed to have a drink with me! We really hit it off from the start.

You know when you were young and watching all those boys meet girl movies and one day you'll hopefully meet yours. I did! This was her – the girl of my dreams! To this day when someone asks, "How did you know?" I reply, "You'll Know!" Many times, people ask me, "I'm going with this girl for a year, and I just don't know if she's the right one for me?" I tell them "If you have to question it – they're not the right one …move on!" I've always believed that if you continue to pursue your dreams and work hard and have faith one day that person will walk right into your life and boy – you will know!

My Hallie's dating, you know exercising her youth. In Geezer language, "Playing the field." I tell her to keep her eye on the donut –not the hole - follow her dreams, work hard to achieve what makes her happy and don't worry about him – he'll come when he's supposed to. He'll walk right in!

Jill walked in my life and I just knew I had found my One. Taking into account all the past drama, I was taking it slow. I have to say, even early on, with Jill I could feel the trajectory of my life changing. Although we never explicitly discussed it, there was an understanding that we would ride a conventional family life into old age. She complimented me and I her. The unspoken word to finish a sentence or a look of understanding, seeing we were on the same page ….so important. Jill, like me, was brought up to work hard. When we met, she was working three jobs, while I was pursuing a career in comedy as well as working during the day in the Garment Center. That now seems so long ago. Quitting my "real job" to plunge into comedy full time, I admit was scary. The insecurity, anxiety of getting gigs. The constant travelling, while having to write authentic new material, along with having to pay the rent and bills? It was tough. Jill made it easy for me. She'd even run through bits (jokes) with me. More importantly, she'd know when I should get my mind away from my circus world. To share a world of love, support, caring, and being together. To refocus, to laugh and look at the world through our lens! I fell in love! We traveled together, laughed together, made love and eventually married.

I say eventually married. We were together a few years when I received an offer to shoot a television sitcom in California - again always respecting other's needs, I asked Jill to come with me to California. She gave me that I know what I need for myself look, then told me, "I'll need a house with a fence, a dog and a car." I smiled, "You got it!" We moved to Santa Monica, California, rented a small house two blocks from the ocean; we bought her a car and shipped mine – ahh let the games begin. No more driving an hour on a good day to Jones Beach in the summer, pay for parking, then walk a mile to get to the beach with freezing water! "Even the seagulls brought lunch and a thermos! "Come on it was just sitting there.

The weather was beautiful, the food was good, the people were shallow, but we were in love, holding hands and going on a new journey together. One day while still in New York, I sensed that something was on her mind. We were walking across the street heading for the movies and all of a sudden she stops walking, looks at me and says, "Ok where are we going?" I knew exactly what she meant. "To the movies? "I offered. She didn't laugh, "You know what I mean – you have until the end of the month to decide. "That was September 18. I waited until September 30, then I asked her to marry me.

With that decision, we went West, and relocated in California. As I pursued my career, Jill opened her own Pilates studio. We put down roots and started a family. So Yes...you can have your cake and eat it too! We purchased our first house. Let's not forget, being circus folk...buying, maintaining and fixing things in a house was the most foreign thing I could imagine. So, this is being a Grown Up!

Don't forget, I grew up in the projects, anything goes wrong, call the super! Jill, on the other hand, growing up in a big Italian family, learned how to fix anything! One day as she was fixing something, she called out, "Bobby get me a Phillips." I ask, "Who's he? Wait. Do we have a secret super?" She shoots me THE look, "Bobby you don't know anything - it's a screwdriver!" I end the exchange with, "So, who's the hammer? Bennie. What about the screw? Is it Suzy? "HELP!

We have two children, Hallie and Madison. Hallie is a typical twenty-eight-year-old hottie – she's smart, and very pretty (Yes, I can be objective.)

Hallie's grown up in another world than I did. I was brought up, work hard, no one is going to give you anything – if you don't have the money, don't buy it, always be a gentleman to women, respect the elderly and especially those with special needs. Where I grew up in Queens, NY, there was a special needs kid in our neighborhood named Julius. My mother told us, "Look out for Julius, don't let people make fun of him or tease him – he needs someone to look out for him. You are that someone." My brother and I did experience times when other kids would tease him and call him retarded or crazy. Of course, we stepped in and protected Julius. We'd make the other kids swear there would be no more name-calling. Occasionally, we had to go as far as physical fighting. What I have learned from life and in particular, these experiences is this. We are all special needs beings in some form or another. Hey look at me!

Our youngest daughter Madison (Maddy) is special needs. She has thrown that door wide open for us. The pure love that this child gives all of us is overwhelming! From the get-go, Jill has taken the "all things Maddy" ball and run with it! Maddy attends the Zeno Mountain Farm Camp. An extraordinary camp for special needs kids and adults. Every summer, for Maddy's first week, Jill is the volunteer Cook for both campers and staff. She is also on the camp Board. While I'm on the road performing, she holds monthly pool parties (which include lunch) at the house, for Maddy's day program. These are in addition to her Saturday night dinners, for both the kids and their aids! It is so hard at times. Finding (and keeping) aides for our daughter, dealing with the schools and agencies for people with special needs, to the task of educating everyday people who encounter my daughter on a daily basis. The respect I have for my wife and the person she has become cannot be easily explained. Very simply – I won!

Of course, there are situations where Jill and I go at it… she's Italian, and I'm a smart-ass comic! She can't stand when I walk the dog at night and have made it a habit to also relieve myself in the alley about a block away from our house. (What can I tell you, my prostate ain't what it used to be!) She screams at me, "Bobby, there are cameras all over the place! You're going to get arrested one of these nights." It only adds fuel to the fire when I answer, "Who cares? I'll wave next time!" Another bone of contention is, sometimes I don't pick up the dog shit my dog deposits around our highfalutin' neighborhood. I think it's my small way of rebelling against privileged people who are smugly, silently flaunting their million dollar, perfectly landscaped yards in my face as I walk by.

Once I was walking the dog and a father and son team were walking their two dogs. I didn't have a leash on my dog and he started to run up to them as I hollered out, "He's friendly!" As I got closer, they were beside themselves about my dog; he's not on a leash, it's against the law, etc. Me, being friendly, told them, "I'm sorry," yet the son kept going and going on. I eventually told them both to shut the fuck up, it's a dog! About a week later at night, the same man was arguing with his wife quite loudly AND SHE WALKED AWAY FROM HIM IN A HURRY! I was in my house, watching from behind the curtains, teasing him, "Nah, nah, nah, nah, nah, nah!" Do people fall into putting up with one another because it's easier? I don't care who I'm with, if I'm not happy, I'm gone! I see friends who I know are in relationships that I'd run from pronto! However, you never know what the situation is or what's going on with their relationship.

Why do people stay together? I know I stay for love, friendship, our beautiful history, fun and laughter. I see so many people who seem to stay together when they shouldn't. They don't look happy, everything out of their mouths to each other is a snap. I couldn't stay with anyone that did not have joy in them.

Jill

Bobby and Jill

Chapter 3

MOM...YOU WERE ALWAYS A PISTOL

•

A MOTHER'S ARMS ARE MORE COMFORTING THAN ANYONE ELSE'S.
-Princess Diana

My mother passed away last year. Margaret Cano Collins was the heart and soul of our family. Some brief background. My mom was raised along with twelve siblings in Shreveport, Louisiana. She met my dad at a USO function. He was an only child from a small town, Swansea, Massachusetts, very educated, a war hero and shy. Along comes this vivacious, beautiful, personable, mixed breed vixen (who had to have known she'd hit pay dirt) and their story begins. If my grandparents were shocked (how could they not be?) by the obvious cultural differences between my parents, in true New England form, it was never discussed.

Growing up, Mom and I had a wild, wonderful (and I'd like to think 'special') relationship! When I was little, I had eye problems. She took me from Queens to an eye clinic in Manhattan. While we were waiting, I told her I had to go to the bathroom. Because I was too young to go alone, she took me to the lady's room. We were waiting for the next available stall. As one of the doors opened, a lady leapt in front of me, and stole my stall! My mother didn't say a word. She motioned for me to step off to the side, lifted her leg and in a blur of accuracy and strength, kicked open the door and grabbed that lady by the arm then literally flung her off the toilet seat and out of the stall! Another time, my brother Roy and I went to the neighborhood store to get a pack of cigarettes for my dad...I think they cost fifty cents! Before we could reach the store, two kids stopped us, hit us and took the money. We ran home, to explain to my mother what had just happened (and why we came back empty handed). As soon as she'd heard what happened, she said, "Get in the car." She circled the neighborhood for what felt like a really long time, searching for them. Thank God, we didn't find them, she would have kicked their asses! There were other car adventures as well. She'd plop me onto the front seat beside her and take off. She became a heat seeking missile, rocketing through the streets, hot on the tail of any vehicle blaring its siren. I'd say, "Mom, I don't think we're allowed to do this!" She'd just laugh and tell me, "Oh Bobby, it's okay they're just showing us some short cuts. We're going to get there really quickly!" We never got a ticket.

We were always laughing, making fun of one another, as well as my brother Roy and my beautiful sister, Dolores. Of course, we never let them hear us. They would have died, if they'd heard the things my mom and I said to each other, or the way we would go after them! We would swear and scream at each other, she'd always threaten me with, "Wait until your father gets home and I tell him how you spoke to me today!" Maybe it was because I was the "baby" of the family, or because the two of us were so similar in our personalities, she never told my father of our antics. Just as I - never shared the times my mom and I would be out walking somewhere and random guys would let out a "wolf whistle" followed by, "Hey good looking!" or "Nice ass! Bring that over here!" to my beautiful mom, with her long black hair and large Kardashian butt. She'd lightly squeeze my hand, "You just 'never mind' keep walking." Out of the corner of my eye, I swear I caught the last glimmer of excitement in her eye, along with her ever so slight smile. I wanted to say something. Hey, I was nine years old. Go ask any guy," How did you feel about your mom when you were nine years old? You're going to get, almost entirely, "Confused!" My mom had a lot going on! I think there just might be a lot of truth woven into the tales about the south. The magic and mystery of the DEEP SOUTH, New-Or-Leenz. My mom was what would have been called today, FIERCE! She had grit and wasn't afraid to show it. She also had her soft and giving side. There was the time I had started working at the department store, Abraham and Strauss (A&S). It took me months to save enough out of my pay, to buy myself a "mock turtleneck" shirt. Finally, I had enough to buy (at the time) a really cool shirt! I was excited, and new to dating. This shirt was to be my ticket into the deep end of the girl pool, and my God, come Friday night, I was going to look good! I came home, showered, and started to dress. I went in the drawer to get the shirt. It was gone, "Mom, where's my new shirt? The one with the mock turtleneck?" Her response, "Oh, the man down the street, you know, the one who works so hard cleaning, I gave it to him, he looked like he needed it. You have two more upstairs." Back to the shallow end.

I learned a lot from my mom. By watching her, I learned how to use humor to diffuse or enhance any situation. To be kind to others, especially those who need to be protected. Learn to listen to your inner voice. I guess you could say mom was my first and best Ringmaster! She showed me life's too short...have Fun while you're here. I love you so much mom and thank-you!

Without a doubt our Mom was the master of the ship. She might not have had much of an education, but she was instrumental in charting each of our lives. During her last years, our visits were less frequent. Primarily because she was in a nursing home in Rhode Island, and I was(mostly) on the west coast in California. I would book myself into places in New England, in order to visit her a couple of times a year. During our last visit, when I looked into her eyes, I instinctively knew how much she missed my father and wanted to be with him. It was time.

I went back to New York. I found a church near our Manhattan apartment, went in and lit a candle. I asked God to take her to, who she always called, "Daddy." For all their contradictions, wildly different backgrounds and struggles, she loved my father very much! The next day my brother called to tell me Mom had passed away. I replied, "She's so happy now, she's with Daddy again."

When I got home, Jill pointed out that my mother's funeral which was to be held in Swansea, Massachusetts (my father's hometown) was now scheduled on the same weekend as a family wedding. Since the wedding had been planned, long before my mother's passing, and was only about twenty minutes from Swansea, we agreed we would skip the actual funeral and instead Jill arranged a luncheon, for family and friends, as a celebration of my beautiful mom's life. This would be a chance to gather, eat, drink and laugh, as we'd toast and share stories of this wonderful woman. This was a way for us to honor my dear mom and attend the wedding. OK, Bobby, strap yourself in, keep your head down and let the drama begin.

The luncheon was wonderful. Friends of my mom, as well as some of my friends were there. One of my friends sharing, "I loved your mom, Bobby. She was always a pistol!" Almost everyone had their favorite story about the lady I called Mom. I listened and laughed, as each divulged a story which defined the woman they knew. I realized just how truly remarkable this woman was, and not just to me. My mom was special to very many people. Each and every one of them called to thank me for inviting them to share in the celebration of her life! I was humbled and so proud!

Now for the low down on the drama. My one brother was so taken aback by Jill putting together that luncheon, and inviting so many friends and relatives, that he let us know, "Bobby, I will not be coming to Jill's luncheon." My other brother sided with him and added his own, "I won't be there either. And just in case you're interested, we plan on having Mom's ashes buried at the cemetery, right after her services." I cannot tell you what it was that had my brothers upset. No idea. I listened to their plan, and trying to remain positive, replied, "That's great, sorry we won't be there. By the way you both missed out on such a moving, and inspirational afternoon. We all laughed and cried as everyone shared a story. I learned things about Mom, I never even knew!" I wanted to say, "You guys know none of this was to be about you two, right? This was all for Mom." Instead, I left it alone, I wasn't going to get into that whole, you know, brother thing. It just made me sad, that we couldn't come together and find comfort in sharing our grief.

I'm going to step away for a minute. My eyes just got a little blurry and I need to clear the lump in my throat. Then I will tell you about how I, not a man of the cloth, or even an internet ordained...anything, came to officiate at my cousin's wedding!

I am not what you would call a wedding guy. First of all, I never attend weddings when they conflict with performances I have already booked. Jill understands (and accepts) I chose this life of a comedian and "The show must go on," is simply a part of that. She will attend, offer my apologies, letting whoever know, "Bobby is sorry he can't be here. He is performing (wherever) and unfortunately, contractually, can't cancel to be here. He sends his Best Wishes!" People always understand!

As you have learned, the luncheon for my mom was to take place on the same weekend one of my cousin's daughters was getting married. Jill and I made the decision to attend. Jill loves weddings! Me? As noted, not so much. However, this funeral/wedding situation was her opportunity to take advantage of my not having a weekend show to work. She made sure I was going to attend! The day before the wedding, the couple learned that their minister could not make it to preside over the ceremony. I swear it was my mom's voice that confidently blurted out, "You know, I was ordained quite a while ago. I could officiate if you need someone?" They overwhelmingly accepted, then suggested, "Let's keep this our secret. We want to see the surprise when our cousin, Comedian Bobby Collins, takes the pulpit!" So that's what we did, I didn't even tell Jill. I showed up at the rehearsal, so I'd at least know where to stand. The next day, I got dressed, (in my ode to Johnny Cash) all in black. Without thinking Jill asks, "What are you doing? Going to a funeral?" Which made us both stop cold. Finally, I said, "Hey Ma? You'd be proud, your baby boy's going to Church!

The bridesmaids and groomsmen filed in first, followed by bride and groom. As I'm walking towards the pulpit, I motion with my arms as I ask, "May we all rise." I take my place behind the pulpit, and loudly begin, "Two Jews walk into a bar..." The crowd goes nuts! I continue having fun, as I make up, religious sounding words, and weave together a ceremony. At one point, the groom stammered and started to tear up. I jumped in with, "It's not too late, you've still got time to run!" I finished up, and announced, "My job here is done. You're married, now let's go eat!! Jill came over to me, "Bobby! You have to tell them the truth. They think you actually married them!" Too late, didn't you hear me say, "You're married?" Besides, with the world the way it is now, what difference is a piece of paper really going to make? Thanks again Mom, for issuing me a license to pretend!

I still do things that my wife can't believe I do. From being influenced by my mother, as well as being an actual comedian, I just can't help myself! I was once waiting at the airport for a flight and I knew I couldn't get on early. All of a sudden, a line of Chinese people on a tour, shows up at my gate, trailing behind a sign instructing them to stay in line. I'm sitting right by the entrance and I can see that the gate agent is already visibly stressed by the people positioning themselves to start boarding. Now there is this huge line of people coming straight toward him, poised to march through his gate. He attempts to speak to them without any success. With a look of desperation (and a touch of fear) he's anxiously searching the faces of everyone, for some type of rescue. In a cry for help, he takes the mic and pleads, "Is there anyone - within the sound of my voice - who speaks Mandarin?" I raise my hand, "I do." He lets out a very loud sigh of relief. Panic quickly returns to his voice as he says to me, "Oh thank goodness. Please. You have to tell them they must wait, until I call out their boarding zone. They must wait for me to call their zone!" I nod in agreement. I move to stand in front of them, and with my best fake Chinese accent proceed to, very animatedly, jibber jabber completely made-up words at them. I finish by raising my hands up to indicate Stop! I extend a courteous waist bow, signaling, this concludes my part of the presentation. That's when I ask the attendant if I might get on the plane now? He smiles gratefully, and says, "Yes." With that I am the first person to board the plane. Score! As the Chinese tour passengers made their way down the aisle to their seats, each one confusingly smiled at me, as they pointed me out to the person behind them. I returned a polite smile, along with, "You're welcome. Always a pleasure to be of help."

I live on planes. So naturally, anything I can do to ingratiate myself to the airlines to obtain early boarding, I'm all over. I have a photo of me, with my head bandaged, wearing a neck brace, lying in the hospital with bruises and tubes coming out from all over my body (It's my souvenir from the time I took a tumble halfway down a mountain in Maine). Anyone looking at this picture would have sympathy immediately. I regularly show this photo to airline personnel while I'm requesting early boarding. It works well, I'm often told, "When the announcement is made to board handicapped passengers, you go get right on." Sometimes I'll joke around and throw in a limp while going to my seat. To this day, Jill is still amazed at the things she's seen me procure "just joking around." with people. I learned from the master, my mom. Life's a stage - have fun! It's not harming anyone.

There are so many times I have assumed the personality of a character, that I become it! I'm from New York. If you can convince New Yorkers that you're someone other than yourself...what's the saying? If I can fake it there, I'll fake it anywhere. Throughout the years, I've lost count of the number of times Jill has said, "How the hell do you always do it?" It's simple, My Momma raised me right!

Margaret Collins

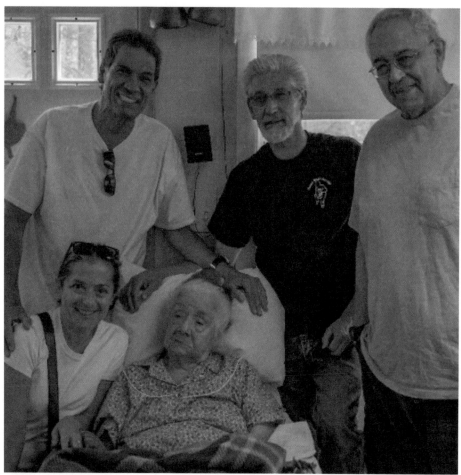

Left to Right Top Row: Bobby, Roy, Tommy
Bottom Row: Jill, Mom

Hallie and Mom

Chapter 4

DIVERSITY

•

WE MAY HAVE DIFFERENT RELIGIONS, DIFFERENT LANGUAGES, DIFFERENT COLORED SKIN, BUT WE ALL BELONG TO ONE HUMAN RACE.
-Kofi Anan

Growing up in New York and using the subway train system was a necessary evil of existence. I still have to explain to people in different parts of the country that a Subway is an underground train, not a sandwich shop. I would have loved to have been picked up by a school bus, or have a parent drop me off or even walk to school. No such luck! Every day my mother would make me the same peanut butter and jelly sandwich wrap it in a piece of curtain or whatever was around, walk me to the Subway entrance and say goodbye and tell me to get to school. I'd say "Mom, I don't want to go down there." She'd tell me, "Bobby, get to school!" A subway was a different world, a world of truths, degradation, knowledge, filth, rodents and bums.

You'd look around on a train and you'd see a myriad of diversity, white businessmen in suits and ties with attaché cases. Whites, Blacks, Puerto Ricans, Chinese, Muslims with their flowing headgear. Hasidic Jews, with tendrils hanging out from under their hats, bobbing their heads in prayer to the rhythm of the train, while their attached waist strings flapped at their sides. Students of all nationalities, everyone starting their day, crammed into a moving train, in a tunnel underground. I'd even see rats bigger than small dogs on the tracks just going about their daily lives. We all got along. It was just what it was. Of course, there was pushing to get inside the fast-closing doors and then fighting for seats. There were the regular beggars asking for money, and the musicians playing for tips in a hat on the platforms. No one would ever put someone down for color, creed, dress or religious affiliation. We were all going about our business, getting to school, work, or praying. We all got along with each other. We all knew when someone was creating a problem - the pervert grabbing a girl's butt, the person taking up two seats, the old lady with the cane standing. People would call-out those offenders for their shit and it was good. Do the right thing! Be kind, be generous, stand up for the unfortunate, be an example to yourself and others. You watched and learned a lot underground, and now you had to take those lessons and apply them to your work, your play, your friends and family. I learned so much, staring into a person's eyes. I'd see what they were hiding and wonder why you would be one way and then be a totally different person on the outside. I learned quickly how people try to appear as someone they are not. The poor, pretending they're rich, the dumb blatantly displaying their ignorance. Why not just be who you are? You can always improve yourself, educate yourself...change! It's just much easier to be yourself.

I remember being on a very overcrowded subway when I felt something in my back pocket. That's when I turned really quickly to grab a guy's hand to catch him with my wallet in his hand. A pickpocket trying to rob me. I don't have a pot to piss in. That's what they do. Grab something and just before the door closes jump out onto the platform. I wrestled him to the ground yelling at him "How could you steal my wallet?" On this very crowded train in New York the people start to form a circle around us. I hear people saying, "Beat him, kill him!" Some people hit him. At the next stop the door opens. He runs out. We're all in this together. We bonded together for the benefit of all. No color, no sides, just the right side. All for one. One for all! That's what it's supposed to be. Pulling no Punches. So, when I see on television where there are groups of people: KKK, White supremacists, White Nationalists, Skinheads, Proud Boys, I stop and say to myself, They would have learned some very valuable lessons on The New York City Transit System.

I grew up in a large family. At dinner if I, or anyone, would make a racist remark or say anything bad about a minority group, we were told to pick up our plate and leave the kitchen. Racist remarks were not tolerated. We were taught to be the example. If we heard something racist or derogatory towards a race. We were taught to speak up against it.

My mother was brought up in the deep South, Shreveport, Louisiana. She married my father, the only child of a fine New England family. They met at a USO dance. She hit gold. It must have been a shock for his parents when my father brought home a mixed-race woman and from a family of twelve siblings. Four were Nuns with one a Mother Superior. Boss of the Nuns. The shit hit the fan! A man of Irish and English descent with roots dating back to Ireland's History, a Collins. Mom's roots went back to a mixed bag of Mexican, Irish, Black and Spanish descendants. Barbequed Irish stew, with some Paella and Tacos on the side.

36

I never knew that mother's lineage had such diversity. Although, I always wondered why I'm the only one in the family who gets such a dark tan, has some serious basketball moves and dances with such ease, mobility and rhythm. Now it all makes sense! People have always questioned my heritage, "You are Italian, aren't you?" or "No, he's Jewish." I'd tell people, I'm Black Irish. It never occurred to me to really find out my roots on my mother's side of the family. I met them only once. People always come over to me and speak Spanish and with my New York education, taking Spanish for five years, I give them, "Hola Isabel como esta?" Now you can see why, when I spent summers in Massachusetts, my grandmother and mother would dress me in such drab colors. They didn't want to draw too much attention to me, so as to start inquisitive adult conversations. Even if their efforts failed, I just ignored the comments. I never allowed rude assumptions to bother me in the least. Little did these ill-mannered cretins know, I was the kid with an older brother who worked summers in New England at a private beach club, where his New York younger brother was allowed to charge food. Which hands down beat sitting on a curb on a hot summer day, sharing cake with their five kids, after playing basketball for three hours. I've been the victim of people's ignorance. Ignorance is easier to excuse than racism.

A girlfriend in college had asked me not to play in my regular Sunday morning basketball game to join her family along with her grandmother for brunch. I reluctantly agreed since they were up visiting from home. I received a phone call five minutes before leaving to join them when my girlfriend tells me on the phone that her grandmother found out I wasn't Jewish, and they preferred me not to come. No basketball, no breakfast. It bothered me that ignorance beat me this time, but it wouldn't again. My family would have welcomed you if you were Black, had one arm, were Muslim with a Chinese accent kicking a soccer ball. I can never figure out why people are taught this? Don't people eventually have to look oneself in the mirror and question? We were brought up to be the example, show yourself first and everyone else the right way. Then if you draw comments and looks, you will know in your heart, you did the right thing. Trust me on this, it will always come back to you as a positive.

As a touring comedian to all parts of this country, I've experienced things in my life that I have used as teaching moments. Like the time I was in the deep South, South Carolina, performing for one of my first corporate shows and paid great money. They put me up in a wonderful hotel suite, provided a limousine, and served the best meals. Yes, that was in addition to the money. As part of the deal, I was to attend a social dress up cocktail lunch party in the afternoon prior to the performance that evening. It was a fancy function with tablecloths, napkins and live music. This is all set in a beautiful area surrounded by a lush creek with cliffs overlooking in the distance. I did notice they were all white except for the help, the waiters and waitresses who were all black. There was the local elite attending: politicians, business leaders, and of course, rich people. Knowing I could fit into any situation with anyone I took in the festivities wholeheartedly. This whole set-up struck me as quite a contrast to other corporate gigs but hey, I'm in the South and do as they do!

Oh, I gotta tell you, these people were boring! They were speaking as though it was enough for just to hear their own voices. I'm standing with a judge, a mayor and a wanna be politician enjoying ourselves making small conversation. I notice some people on the cliff in the distance above the creek and I say "Wow, there are people up there overlooking the water, so cool." The response that followed, in a very matter-of-fact tone, was unsettling. The mayor said, "Oh, that's where the niggers stay." I could tell by the ease in which he used the N word, it was part of his everyday vocabulary. Oh, not today! I responded, just as matter-of-factly, "My wife's a nigger." The speed at which those 3, "Fine southern gentleman," departed my side almost knocked me over! After my performance, which felt like it went off well, I was never invited back again. I tell this story because it felt SO good putting a racist in his place!

I see so many people that look to the size of their bank accounts, where they live, or titles, to make themselves feel successful or superior. They define themselves by what they have, not who they are. I understand that discrimination exists, but it still rocks me when it is so blatant. No, my wife's not black, just a very hairy Italian woman. We vacuum a lot. But, when we are placed in situations where you must call out the bigot, knowing full well that the push back will be strong, you will feel so right for throwing that punch. Just maybe, those people need a kick in the ass to wake up and see what damage they do for no good reason. It would have been so much easier to ignore the man's comment then later, in a safe environment, tell my friends of this crap that still exists, right out in the open. I realize things come into our lives for reasons. Then we are tested to see how honestly, we handle them.

Growth brings change. Change doesn't always bring growth. Situations are placed in our paths for reasons. How we handle them speaks to what kind of a person we really are. Afterwards you will look back and you will see if you were honest, had integrity, showed your faith and have a stronger purpose in life. Standing on a stage and looking into an individual's eyes I get to see where they are coming from. The way people respond to humor speaks a lot about themselves. Those are the times I try to use my humor to offer another point of view that makes sense and can possibly push the love needle.

What do you with dumb? Since they don't know they are dumb can they be helped? Maybe they are not so far away from not being dumb. You know, maybe they just need a little nudge towards the smarter edge. Maybe you can say something that will make them see the light. Of course, they were brought up to be dumb. Not their fault. It's an acquired trait. Being a racist is taught. They didn't wake up one day and say, damn, get that Mexican piece of shit away from my property. They've heard it through family or friends. Someone laughed in approval and that made it acceptable. If they hear others laugh at how stupid it is to be a bigot, maybe it will begin to move the smart needle a bit. To be sure - Nigger, Spick, Chink, Camel Jockey, Wop, Kike, Jungle Bunny, are samples of the divisive, ugly, hurtful daily verbiage for kids of my generation. We heard it all - daily, growing up in the city. But that was then - this is now! The time has come for all of us to hold up the mirror, and take collective, as well as individual, responsibility for the damaging reflection. We can no longer ignore and allow such hurtful, ugly language to be thought of as acceptable. This is no longer who we are. We must do better if we hope to be better.

I was watching a Neo-Nazi march on television, white people with weapons carrying tiki torches reciting, "Jews will not replace us!" With what? JOBS! You are marching against the ones who provide jobs - morons. Those people did not win at genetic roulette. We are a country of immigrants from all over the world. My ancestry and yours. Why would these white racists think they were better than anyone else? They listened to a President who basically sides with them exposing his ignorance and racist overview. Are you kidding me, not in my United States of America!! This is not who we ARE – WE'RE PAST THIS! Is this the backlash from having an intelligent black President for eight years? Oh, come on! We're better than this. I love the fact that people can finally see they're so-called

Politicians for who they really are. SPINELESS enablers! Remember when Government shut down? I'm from New York. Again, we didn't even know it was open!

Let's invite them down to the subway system and change their minds about division and hate! In my career, I've met so many politicians, you shake their hands and immediately you want to clean yourself with a chicken! We tend to forget our government; these politicians are paid to work for us. They said vote for me, trust me and I will represent you. I don't remember giving the government a leave of absence when it shut down. Then you turn on television. Television, the dumbing down tool in America and see the mass shooting in Sandy Hook Connecticut. Twenty-one little angels were killed, and no one has, then or now, done anything about stopping crazy people from getting guns. No requirement at all. Just have the money. Are you kidding me? That's when I gave up believing that the government made any sense. Pay your taxes, wear a helmet … stay low. One Hundred and fifty-four mass shootings just in 2018 alone. Two hundred and eighty-four in 2019, nothing done. Don't let anyone or anybody tell you that America is not the most wonderful, greatest place on Planet. The freedom, the diversity, the love, the intelligence makes up who we are. Okay, I'm going off on one of those rants you see on TV, sorry. But when I see people acting like Neanderthals, I want to shove their noses in shit and say, "Sniff, smell, okay don't do it again! Grow up!" They should be carrying around signs that read, "Look into my eyes. This is what dumb looks like. Someone please help me!"

Ok, one more, then I'm finished! PEOPLE - are you kidding me. I'm just amazed that people can't see the hypocrisy of what they're saying. And why no one is saying to them, "OK this has got to end - You're Fired! Now Go home and play nice!"

Keep in mind, we bring to the table a vast variety of life – embrace it, learn from it, pass it on the right way. I see many people who hear things that have been said, or referred to in conversation with friends or family, and then repeat what they heard to others. Then say they are amazed that the person said it, rather than injecting something at the time. Speak up! Never be afraid of doing or saying the right thing. It will always come back to aid you in the positive manner, a great feeling. When I am on stage, I will sometimes speak to people who are showing their insecurities and offer them the opportunity to see life in a more open way. Thank God! I still hear from people I know who rationalize their own truths and place it out there for discussion or others who just place it out there to show their ignorance.

I live in Santa Monica, California, as well as New York City. There was looting in the streets of Santa Monica. People were breaking store windows and helping themselves to whatever they could grab up. My black friends, the ones I grew up with, called me and asked me if I was all right! We discussed how it was growing up when we were young. The police were pricks and would use their so-called power against us. We were hit and called names all the time by the cops. We played nice in front of them, but we hated them. We also spoke about the kids we went to school with who were the dopes, the losers. We also talked about those kids who were bullied and made fun of. How those were the ones who later became police officers, grew up to now carry guns and use their badge and uniform as a power trip. Again, not all the police are "damaged goods" but too many of them are. Another old friend who was a New York police officer, went on to become a bigshot in the Florida Police department. He reminded me of the might of Police unions. He knows should officers commit a crime against a citizen they would be well protected by the union... to sweep anything under the carpet. Which is why 2 days of desk duty and then back on the job, business as usual, can no longer be tolerated. Those who are insecure about themselves, must not be kept in a position to violently violate another human, in an effort to elevate their own skewed ego.

David Chappelle

Yakof Smirnoff

Paul Rodriguez

Chris Rock

Chapter 5

I PLEDGE ALLEGIANCE...
WITH LIBERTY AND JUSTICE FOR ALL

●

I HAVE LOBBYISTS THAT CAN PRODUCE ANYTHING FOR ME. THEY'RE GREAT.
-Donald J. Trump

I travel throughout this United States every weekend, making people laugh, to look at themselves, to actually see themselves and hopefully, through laughter, show them another way to look at life. Remember when the government shut down? Again I'm from New York...we didn't even know it was open! I see more people mad and angry now-a-days than ever before. People in Iowa are giving you the finger. People all over are uncomfortable, angry and confused, you can feel it out there! I've found myself in the car, honking at people and giving them my high beams. I've found myself anxious and impatient. My wife has pointed this behavior out to me. I've been short and ready to cut people off in the middle of whatever they're talking about. Not nice. Not me! People are watching television, CNN, MSNBC, Fox News, now more than ever.

My wife went to the Women's March when Donald Trump became president, I asked her at the time, "What's up?" Her response, "I'm not going to allow any person, not even the President of the United States, to make fun of a special needs person." Politics, break it down. Poly, what's a poly? An expensive trained bird who repeats everything you say. What's a tick? A blood-sucking insect. Polytick = politics.

People, it's all about the money, pay your taxes, stay low. When I say it's all about the money, let me explain. How many times have you and I heard about that altruistic person who wants to change what they see as our country heading in the wrong direction, and decides to become politically active, to bring about change. Well guess what? It takes money to run for any kind of political position in our country today. When you realize the $100 you've collected from your family and friends, ain't going to cut it, you look for ways to fund your campaign. So, when you're approached, with the promise of millions, for your "do good" plan, what do you do? You jump on it. Only to discover, you just sold your soul to the NRA or some other organization for money. They now own you. So much for your ideals, common sense, truth, honesty, and integrity now!

I have always wondered, who in their right mind would pursue a career in politics? I was brought up to honor our country. To respect its people, and the Constitution. To trust in the balance of power. I was taught to - treat everyone as equal, help the less fortunate, practice love over hate, give with no expectation of receiving, respect my parents, and treat people the way I want to be treated (equally.)

I've always been proud to be an American citizen. Sure, I've heard the racist comments, I've seen the less fortunate being stepped on. I've heard all the righteous rhetoric i.e., "A country is only as strong as its weakest link." But now the anger is boiling over here in our country. I was brought up to be the optimist, to see the bigger picture – don't get caught up in the snapshots. However, this past year has me wanting to scream out, "This is not who we are!"

People blame former president Donald Trump and his administration. I say, he's a symptom not the cause. We all have a part in this cause. You and I, for standing on the sidelines and watching it all unfold, rather than getting involved with our words and actions, being the right examples to one another. I try. I stand on a stage and hold up a mirror and with my words, hopefully through laughter, show people who we are and where we are heading. We have many issues: #MeToo movement, Black Lives Matter, women's equality, abortion issues, immigration, separating families, inequality of taxation, racism, lies and deceit. Do these exist? You bet. Will we all come out looking and feeling better off than when it started? You bet we will. The correction is in! What do you call a president who lies, obstructs, has no transparency, plays people against each other, bait-and-switches all the time, sides with racism, treats women like objects, tries to divide us, and draw us to the dark side? In New York, we call that person a punk, a loser, a con artist. He's the kid who takes his basketball and leaves if he's not chosen in the game. We kick him as far as we can and tell this asshole, "Never come back!"

Hey, don't think I'm so naïve. I see people around this country who can't even fill out a food stamp application. Let's keep in mind the majority of people in our country have a seventh grade reading level! (Add broken education system to the list.) They've been left out of the whole system. Politics is something "over there" in Washington. They feel the whole system has ignored them. They are looking for someone, anyone to include them. I heard them say, "That Donald Trump, he was the host of a television show for six years, he's a billionaire, he's going to make America great again." Wow! Trump appealed to a base who felt he was "the man" and spoke with their voice, and yet they failed to see he was running the country like a reality show! Who makes you swear your loyalty to them and makes you sign a confidentiality agreement? What was he hiding?

He was also guilty of defending symbols of the Confederacy, race-baiting through a national crisis, denying the objective realities of a pandemic, speaking of how to "grab the pussy "of women, and making fun of special needs individuals. People, open up your eyes and your mouths and respond! Based on my upbringing in New York, you could look into a person's eyes and see what they're hiding. I'm still surprised that people watch television and can't see the bullshit, never mind.

I watched Donald Trump as president and I found him comical. If I was to know a person like Trump – a friend or neighbor – I would say to him, "Hey you're seventy-four years old and your hair is the color of Tang! And by the way, your hair is combed over from one side to the other, making your worst enemy the wind! It's time to accept your aging process and stop with the spray tan! Cut the hair, shape it to a natural aging white hair classy look, not a comb-over orange dyed color, looking like an emoji! Got it?! Now do it!"

Was not anybody talking to him? It was so obvious that he was doing this all for himself. Doing it for money, not for the uneducated who believed he cared for them and would look out for them. Please! Did people really believe what he was spouting? Did he really believe what he was saying? Statements like... bring the military into major cities to contain crime, drink bleach disinfectant to heal the coronavirus. Don't forget he pardoned his friends, who stood by him, who plead guilty of crimes against the country. His continued feed into political conspiracy theories to shore up his base. Sad but true! He tried to get the governor of Georgia to change the voting numbers to appeal to his base and he lied about a "rigged election." In the same week, he encouraged an insurrection march against our national capitol where five people were killed! When someone elbows you in the head playing in a street basketball game, you warn him and if he should do it again, you take him out! Time to leave this fool before he attempts to place our country in harm's way! Are we not seeing the bigger picture here or are we allowing this person and his group of losers to lead us down a path to a despotic, autocratic, dictatorial rule!

Other countries are looking at us and saying, "What the hell happened to you? You have always been the pinnacle of democracy, an example to the world!"

I've always been amazed at people who could get blinded by money. On stage, I point this out. Dumb people don't know they're dumb! When you're dead, you don't know you're dead. Other people feel the pain. Same thing when you're stupid. I'd like to believe, most people see Trump and ask, "How can this narcissistic, shallow, dumb, racist, sociopathic person explode on our scene, in our country, bullying others, lying, baiting, threatening and dividing our country, all for his own pocket! Wow, getting that out was so satisfying!

Now, let's look and laugh at what's really out there to fix. First and foremost is the pandemic and the economic crisis, as well as race relations. We must all help each other calm down. The anxiety in our country is so thick, you can cut it with a knife. We're all in this together. Let's educate each other rather than yell and scream, "Where's your mask?" Red, blue, right, left. I went to the post office yesterday and (not thinking) I forgot my mask in the car. I walked into the post office, got in line and some guy yelled out loud, "Where the hell is your mask?" I'm ready to scream back at him. There's a nice way to speak to someone and then there's your way, then I realized, I was the one he was screaming at! I apologized nicely to him and the rest of the line, went out to the car and retrieved my mask. I come back and he's still on edge but has moved toward the normal side.

People ask me all the time, "Hey Bobby, do you discuss politics in your shows?" Of course, I do. I'm a comedian. My job is to make people laugh and just maybe show people a different viewpoint from theirs. I can stand on the stage and see the wheels turning from what I just said and they're laughing at it and allowing it to register. I was once performing in Birmingham Alabama and some woman in the balcony hollered out, "Hey Bobby, what do think of Donald Trump?" Without a beat, I reply, "There's a reason why they let John Hinckley out early." You could have heard a pin drop. I continued, "You don't think another prisoner ran over to John's cell and said, "Word's out - Donald Trump has a tattoo of Jodie Foster on his chest!" After the show, two well-to-do couples came over and asked me, "Bobby, was that true? Donald Trump has that tattoo?" You people are idiots... get off the planet! Another time, I was working in a large theater, talking about politics. One person, out of twelve hundred. started yelling out in the middle of my show, "That's it Bobby Collins, goodbye Bobby

Collins, goodbye…." I stop, watch him leaving, still yelling on his way out, then comment, "Ignorance can be educated, crazy can be medicated, but there's no excuse for stupid!" The audience laughed, applauded and we went on! Once at a private performance in wealthy Naples, Florida. I'm on stage, showing both sides of the political circus, when one man, well known to everyone there, stands up and yells out. "Why don't you take your liberal ass back to California?" My response, "Dad? Dad, is that you?" They laugh and we go on. Like I've said many times, we're sharing the planet with a lot of different types of people, we have to start thinning out the herd, the gene pool could use some chlorine!

I've performed at many political functions, I've met many politicians, you shake their hands- again you want to clean yourself with a chicken! Yes, I know, there are some who are very altruistic and care for our country; but I'm from New York and from where I was brought up, it's a money corporation. A place where you can plainly see especially now - it's used as a fake excuse to make money. People pay your taxes, listen to your heart, and see through the bullshit and the misinformation. I was talking recently about politics and about the misinformation given with the QAnon conspiracy and the lies. I'm still amazed at the amount of people in our country who follow this crap! What you see on the news is not always the truth. Be the example for yourself and your family. I 've performed in front of two presidential functions - both democratic and republican…money doesn't discriminate, people do. I was contracted to perform (after Trump was, elected) at Trump Golf Course. My wife was so concerned, "You're not going to do your political shtick, are you? You could get a lot of jobs and money out of this opportunity. Just do your act." I smiled. She knew. I'm a comedian, you have to tell the truth through humor and be the person who you are. You touch subjects that have a vast effect on all of us and you see people laugh and maybe, just maybe… you can get them to see another point of view! Through laughter! My opening line was, "Welcome everyone, we have a new president now. I guess, Orange is the new Black."! Everyone laughed and applauded.

I've known Donald Trump for years. I've worked at comedy venues in Florida and at his (then) three casinos in Atlantic City, on bills with Julio Iglesias, Dolly Parton, Cher and others. I recently played the Atlantic City Hard Rock Casino, which was formerly Donald Trump's Taj Mahal Casino (before the government closed it down). I was about to go on stage and the opening act still had about ten minutes left. I was standing next to the stage operator and we started talking. I said to her, "Okay, I'm going to throw a name out to you - Donald Trump." She whipped off her headphones, looked me straight in the eye and emphatically stated, "That son-of-a-bitch." She told me the government came in and informed him he owed something like sixty million dollars in back taxes from his three casinos, and that if he didn't pay up, they would close him down. If you believe - that this man - you elected President, really cares about the working man; two days later, thirty-one hundred people... were out of work! Sad but true. Money is some people's GOD. He only cares about his brand - Trump.

I do my best to find the humor in what's happening in our country. I know it's hard with family, employment, sickness, the news; but we'll all get through this! Be the example and remember "The Cream rises to the top and shit floats for a while before it sinks." People, the shit is sinking!

Laurence O'Donnell

Wolf Blitzer

Colin Quinn

Dan Rather

Chapter 6
THINK P.I.G.

●

PERSISTENCE, INTEGRITY, AND GUTS...
INGREDIENTS FOR A SUCCESSFUL BUSINESS & SUCCESSFUL LIFE.
-Linda Chandler

There are many times as a hard-working comedian traveling this vast country when I'm asked, "Why do you take certain jobs?" Sometimes I ask myself the same question. Then I remember, this is what I signed up for. I remember when I was first starting my comedy career, I took jobs for the time and experience spent on stage, definitely not the money! I spend time creating and practicing new material, working out timing, the rhythm and the order of presentation. I have to remove myself from my material and view it from a distance to ensure a performance that is cohesive, relevant and informative. I watch many comedy performances and see how the flow is disrupted by not seeing the whole picture of what that comic is trying to relay. Not my job to fix it, but it is my job to see the patterns and flow of my own material and make sure it is smooth.

Nowadays, I am in a position to accept the occasional performing job below my pay grade. I take these gigs, primarily for extra stage time (you're only as good as your last performance) also, they provide a place to work out any kinks from my material. These less paying spots meet both of those goals! I had some people the other night ask me, "Bobby, why is an A-list comic like you working in a shithole (their term...but they weren't wrong!) like this, with only about three hundred people?" I tell them it's not about the money or the venue; it's what I need to master the material, to work out the order, the cohesiveness and the rhythm of the flow so I can continue to be an A-list comic and perform in front of huge theater crowds. I remember the $15 sets when I was starting out, running around and doing at least four sets a night to perfect my material (and make enough money to get home.) I listened to all the bullshit from comedy club owners and the complaints from other comics. Keep your eye on the donut – not the hole. I heard them and moved on. I always took the best and left the rest.

I was not the type of comic who would hang around other comedians. I was friendly and kind but would do my work and move on to another venue to learn. I used to hear other comics say, "Oh Bobby, great guy, great comic, but as soon as he's off the stage he's gone." Jerry Seinfeld, Drew Cary, George Wallace, Richard Belzer, Richard Lewis, Richard Jeni, Eddie Murphy, Roseanne Barr, Ray Romano, Larry David, Brad Garrett, Chris Rock, Lewis Black and Dave Chappelle are all great comedians. People who I have the utmost respect for and the pleasure to have known. If we worked together over the years at different gigs, that's when I would laugh, hang out, and be friends with them. People forget, this is a business and I am at these venues, first and foremost...to work!

I'll give you an example. There are times when I'll take a comedy job for the money of course. However, there are venues, in locations, that I'll book as a personal perk! As when I've been working on the road for a few weeks and now I have an opportunity to work in Lake Tahoe, CA (God's country.) Hey, I'm from New York, living in California and New York, so when I am offered the opportunity to perform up in Lake Tahoe in the summer, I'm going to take it. Here's my opportunity to enjoy the beauty of the place, have some fun and get away from the rest of the world to think and write new material – you bet I will go! Last night, I headlined in Lake Tahoe at the Improv Comedy Club in Harvey's Casino. An MC opens the show, he mentions we had previously worked together in Boston. He's a nice guy, a good comedian (he opens with ten minutes, the featured act does twenty and I do an hour.) Fun, easy, right? It's the second night of five and the audience is very vocal and shouting out to the MC. It happens! The MC calms them down, proceeds with his set and brings on the featured act, I'm sitting backstage with the featured act and he is understandably, freaking out about the crowd yelling. I tell him, just stay in your act, don't chase them, allow them to come to you. You're the professional. The guy is a young and upcoming comic who is talking about fucking and doing cocaine, asking the audience questions. In short, doing everything he shouldn't do. He goes over his time, the director is pissed off, the audience is yelling at him. As a comedian, you always have to KNOW your audience, smart, dumb, old, young, right, left. I always peep out from behind the curtains to see who I'm performing for! Know your audience. The feature was demoted to ten minutes instead of twenty and the MC will pick up his time and probably get more money for it. Ahh, the lessons of Lady Stage. He'll learn! Comics ask me all the time to watch their sets and if I could give them some advice or criticism that maybe I've learned along my path. I inform them I would (if I like them) yet in the past I've been asked to critique a show and the person who asked me afterwards got all prissy and annoyed at me for telling him or her what I thought he might want to change or add to their show. Don't ask if you're not going to listen and either try my advice or not!

Allowing people to see who you are just adds to the whole presentation and makes it that much funnier. Once, a very good comic who dressed in jeans and a t-shirt and had a beard and mustache asked me, "What am I not seeing, I can't seem to connect with audiences?" It was plainly obvious to me! I nicely tell him, "You're working on a stage, which is quite literally above people and they have to physically look up to you. What they see is a funny man hiding from himself and the audience. Cut all your facial hair and dress better. You can always go back to it!" A few months later, I ran into him - no facial hair, dressing like an adult. He thanked me because he noticed a complete difference in how he performed and the audience's reaction to him. Always help a fellow comic out!

I'm asked to participate in many charity events. I do, of course, because of my own special needs daughter, Madison. However, I have to keep in mind I am a business. There are times when I'm asked to perform charity events, and I can't due to the fact I'm already booked at a paying venue. Many times, future jobs come out of performing at these events. That's a plus! Every year my daughter goes to a summer camp, Zeno Mountain Farm, which is composed of ninety-five special needs people from all over the country. They come together and support each other and have the time of their lives, laughing, swimming, performing in a play, going to sporting events and just enjoying one another's company. It truly is magical! We've put on a comedy benefit event called "Comics for a Cause "for the last fifteen years. All the most well-known comedians participate: Jay Leno, Ray Romano, Bill Burr, Billy Gardell, Paul Raiser, Dave Atell and Arsenio Hall to name a few. It truly is a night to remember. It's our own charity event for the camp. No one pays to attend Zeno Camp. I know for a fact many of the families would never be able to afford such an all-inclusive experience. Campers and their families wait a year with such excitement in anticipation to return each year. To see the look on their faces, brings such joy to my heart. To see my daughter who can't walk very well or speak, with the biggest smile on her face, brings tears to my eyes and I thank God for her!

Recently I did a Zoom graduation commencement speech for a special group of graduates. It was so much fun and, especially during the pandemic, quite rewarding for me as well! I spoke about the lessons I learned in life and how I overcame so many obstacles. I mentioned the importance of what's inside a person, how it's the quality of one's character and not what's seen on the outside. After wrapping up my speech - I unzipped my graduation robe and walked off in my underwear! They loved it!

I'm asked to do so many different types of presentations. Ranging from: Many different organizations, performing at various companies fun corporate events, to lending my skills performing for causes that touch my heart. Of course, events for children with special needs, as well as raising funds for service dogs, in addition to fire and police organizations, raising money to help their communities. When I can't give of my time (because of previously contracted commitments) I always try to give a donation. Hey, we're all in this together! I remember growing up poor and when it came to supporting charities... We were always taught that charity begins at home!

Billie Gardell

Arsenio Hall

Jerry Seinfeld, Jim Gaffigan and Bobby

Smokey Robinson

Robert Klein

Chapter 7
FOR MY BROTHER, TOMMY

●

WHEN SOMEONE YOU LOVE BECOMES A MEMORY,
THE MEMORY BECOMES A TREASURE.
-Linda Chandler

Okay, it's been four months since I last performed. In my forty years of performing this has never happened! I've never been off more than a week here and there. The world is going through a Pandemic – people across the globe are catching a deadly virus and thousands are dying daily. There's civil unrest in our country which hopefully, will create a new landscape in our county, for both acceptance and equality. What's next Jumanji?

Suddenly having so much time on my hands, I've been doing a retrospective of my life...where I am, events and people who have shaped me and what I find irksome. Along the way, I've found out things about my own life that I never knew! I grew up with two brothers and one sister. I was the youngest of us four, and I like to think the best looking! Come on – it was just sitting there. My parents first born was my brother Tommy, who was brought up by my grandparents. I always thought it was so strange, when my parents left Massachusetts to move to New York City, Tommy remained in New England with my grandparents - permanently. What little information I was able to gather about...why(?) I got from my sister. Without a lot of detail, she informed me that because she and Tommy were so close in age (11 months apart) the prospect of raising four children was too much for our mom to handle. So, the decision (made before I was born) was Tommy (the oldest) would be raised by our paternal grandparents. Being the youngest, this arrangement was just the way it had always been. I never asked my parents why Tommy never came back with us after our family summer visits. Every summer we would all escape the hot muggy summers in the City, where there were no beaches or swimming (only an occasional trip to Jones Beach on Long Island). I'd spend my days playing basketball, on hot asphalt courts with the guys, then sit sweating on the curb, eating crap. Summer would officially begin when we would make the trip to spend time in Massachusetts with my grandparents and my brother. I loved it! Their place had massive trees, and a long driveway that

65

wound its way up to the house on a large corner plot of land. They had a chicken coop, a huge barn, a big vegetable garden and cats and dogs. The bonus was getting to spend time with my big brother - I loved spending time with him, he was smart, athletic, intelligent and funny! Tommy had a huge, all to himself bedroom, on the second floor of my grandparents' house. I would tell him stories about how it was to share a bedroom (the size of his bathroom) with my brother Roy. I would tell Tommy what a great place this was, a place I would have loved to grow up in... And he did!

Every night at six pm my grandmother would ring a bell and everyone in the house, my Aunt, Uncle, Grandparents, all three of us, my parents and Tommy, would come down for an unbelievably delicious dinner! Which is why I would always tell Tommy how we ate at home – fried bologna with corn griddles and apple sauce. Our dinners were always terrible! So, I learned early on to ingratiate myself with my friends' parents, then go over to their houses to partake in their dinners. You've heard of "Sing for your supper?" Well, I would make other families laugh for mine! Recently, I was speaking with my brother Roy, and we both agreed how bad our mother's cooking was. How much more we enjoyed our school's cafeteria food. I can remember telling Tommy, "For thirty-five cents (including two milks) Roy, myself and Delores, considered lunches served at school to be fine dining." I think Tommy thought I was kidding!

The place in Massachusetts, where Tommy grew up was a small town named Swansea. He attended the local school and excelled in both academics and athletics. He was captain of the basketball team, and co-captain of the football team. He was also voted most popular. A few times we got to watch him play at the school's small stadium, which would be packed. He was the star! I would say to others seated by us, "That's my brother. Tommy Collins, he's, my brother." I was so proud of him! He was the one who inspired and motivated me to also play and excel at basketball. Tommy was my hero. However, I could always tell... I would see it in his eyes, there was something, something missing in him. He carried some type of chip (maybe more like a nugget) on his shoulder, his whole life. I'm no shrink, but being separated from your parents and siblings, growing up as the kid who was basically, "given away" is bound to take a toll. I would always try to let him know, "Tommy, you're not 'missing out' on anything." I'd explain how we lived in housing projects, and small apartments, with nut job, alcoholic, neighbors. Our neighborhood was composed of poor people. The topics of conversations were always about the troubles of one or another neighbor, or whose family member just overdosed (or died) of this or that! I also learned recently, from my sister and my other brother, that Tommy didn't really like my parents all that much. Hey, can't say I blame him! I would not be fond of the people who separated me from my family and deprived me of growing up with a sister and brothers. The flip side is...he would have been such a great role model for us! I think sometimes that's why he drove himself to excel, he was proving his worth (to our parents, himself, and others). Tommy never married and again I've always wondered why? Was it because his own family had given him up, that he felt he wasn't good enough to raise a family of his own? Sadly, I will never have the opportunity to finally ask these (and other) questions. My brother Tommy died this past year from Covid-19. He was a diabetic, his numbers had risen to such a high level, he needed to go to the hospital. He was tested for Covid-19 when he was admitted and tested negative. He remained in the hospital until his numbers came down...one day. A few days after he was released, my brother Roy stopped by his apartment to check up on him. He found Tommy in his apartment, unconscious, sitting in front of his computer. He was rushed to the hospital, admitted and died a week later of Covid 19. Tommy's death struck me, my brother and sister very hard! Since his death, I've spoken to a few of his friends, who knew him well. These were friends that I'd been introduced to through the years, having come with my brother to watch me perform, when I was in his area of the country. We'd always have a good time, laughing and telling stories together. I was so touched when these friends relayed just how very proud my brother was of me. I never knew that and hearing this made me feel wonderful!

Boy could my brother talk on the phone! We'd cover everything from the Celtic's upcoming season to what photos he was taking for the fantastic calendars he was working on (he always sent me one). He and his circle of friends were such accomplished photographers. I miss having those conversations. There were times when he'd be talking so much, I'd put the phone down...go take a shower, then run grab a "to go "dinner, come back pick up the phone, and he's still talking! That's Tommy!

I've learned a lot since his passing and am so glad I reached out to his friends. I've heard how he touched people through his photographs, as well as his personality, charisma, and charm. I love you, Tommy!

I've always taken the high road in life, whatever the situation or whoever the person involved was. I've performed in so many different venues, be it, theaters, clubs, private shows or large formal events, as well as for politicians and large corporations. I've seen people from all sides of life – rich, poor, smart and dumb. I have always done my job to the best of my abilities. Have I had to learn to adapt to different situations? You bet I have! However, I've always remained my own person. Hopefully allowing people to see themselves through my comedy and maybe - just maybe, change their outlook on life. My brother was that way too. Whatever hurt or disappointment he felt inside, a void of not having a traditional family growing up, the closeness, guidance and love of two parents, or sharing in the fun and silliness of his brothers and sister – he rose above all that. He became a positive example to all he touched. I think we've all seen or known families where there's one kid who didn't take the high road, and the pain and repercussions that followed. The psychological trauma, the depression, the drugs, the counseling, and in some cases, the attempted (sometimes successful) suicides. Not Tommy – he rose above it all to show himself and the rest of all of us the Right way.

Okay, now that I got that out (not without a tear or two). It's time for this New York kid to scream and take this to the next (liable) level. The anger that I feel about my brother's death (as well as so many other deaths) because of this administration's complete and utter lack of leadership, is incalculable! From the onset of this horror, I've seen very clearly how the pandemic was handled. Terribly! The misinformation, lies, ignorance and division; all for selfish, personal gain of one man, over the protection of all citizens of this great nation. NO! Not in my country! I taught high school US foreign policy and have seen the map laid out of countries where its leaders followed this same toxic pattern: division of public information, turning on people who are not loyal to the leader, changing the rule of law to conveniently suit their objectives; bait and switch the lemmings, flat out lie, cheat and do whatever it takes to perpetuate and protect their megalomaniacal regime!

Accountability is something that has been completely absent during #45's term, which is why – I was considering bringing a Civil Lawsuit against the President of the United States, Donald J. Trump for the death of my brother George Thomas (Tommy) Collins for Negligence, Fraud, Wrongful Death, Breach of Fiduciary Duty and Involuntary Manslaughter.

Note: Since I wrote this chapter, we've held (and survived) a Presidential Election; I feel a US Civics reminder might be in order. We live in a country based on a Constitution. A nation Of the People, By the People, For the People. The government works for us...we are not the subjects of our government. Our public office holders (from school boards to President of the United States) ARE ELECTED. We pay the salaries of our elected government officials; they work for us. If a duly elected government official proves to be detrimental for the people, then it is the right of the people and by the people, to elect a replacement for the betterment of all people of the United States.

God Bless America!

George (Tommy) Collins

Tommy

Chapter 8
ANXIETY

●

YOU CAN'T STOP THE WAVES, BUT YOU CAN LEARN TO SURF.
-Jon Kabat-Zinn

I find myself getting ahead of myself lately – I'm short with people, I cut them off when they're talking, I don't want to hear their whole song and dance. I find myself easily getting angry at people. I honk the car horn a lot lately. I've become very aggressive with people. This is not who I am! I can sense the anxiety around the country and on television. I'm the person who addresses this on the stage, turns it around and let people see themselves and laugh. Am I becoming one of them? I'm worrying about money and work now more than ever. Then I think about the three theaters where I recently worked, and the three standing ovations I received. Which helps me bring it down, to calm myself.

As a comedian, it is only natural that I worry about money and supporting my family. I don't have a 9 to 5 job, with a regular paycheck, benefits and vacation time. I am my own boss, booking and travel agent. It's up to me to find places to perform, then to negotiate my pay. I've been doing this over thirty-five years! To be honest, I've done well. When Hallie was little, she would ask me, "Daddy, are we rich?" I would smile and say, "You're not...but I'm doing okay." Even so, deep inside, I'm always going to be that poor kid from Queens. Subconsciously, I'm always telling that kid to keep quiet. I don't know, maybe the energy needed for that constant inner conversation keeps my motor running at a higher frequency. But come on! This is different, I'm outwardly more anxious than ever. I was always the example, I'd evaluate the problem, settle on a course of action, and move on. However, now I feel like I am in a state of "high alert" all the time. I see the direction our country is heading and don't like it. I see the rise in racism, the poor getting poorer, the me-too movement. I see immigration demonized, foreign children being kept in cages, our constitution used for its own play, truth stretched to the limit, the lies, the misinformation, the cowards who don't take a stand and speak up, the rationalizations dummied up. This is not who we are!

71

In the past I could always see the correction coming and felt that balance would be restored. I'd be the one reassuring others, "Don't worry things are going to change." Now though, for whatever reason, it's taking a longer time, I'm not seeing a change, and this makes me angry! It seems every day we read about, children falling behind in their education, actresses cheating to get their kids into elite colleges, investment firms being investigated for illegal trading. We're subjected to a never-ending stream of name calling, fact hiding, bullshit, bullying, slander, for what? It's like everyone's forgotten kindness, discussion, friendship, sharing, integrity, giving, and love!

I remember as a kid, we'd settle things with a spirited game of Rock, Paper, Scissors, or use our fingers, throwing out odds/evens. If it were a really important decision, we'd step it up to two out of three. If you won, great, if you lost you lost and everyone accepted that, no hard feelings, and you went back to what you were doing! Just writing down my thoughts, is starting to help me feel better. The tension in my neck and shoulders is lessening. So, I'm thinking, I'm just going to go with this. But I have to tell you, I'm still in favor of fixing a lot of the world's problems (and my own) with simple childhood games. Seriously...it couldn't hurt! If nothing else, it brings back great memories. When I was growing up the picture was very clear! When I'd get stuck in life, I'd always be able to look around or inward, to find something to help guide me. Not so much lately. I'm feeling stagnated, like I'm being pressed against a wall, something is blocking my mental view. What is it? It's everything! We are living in a very real Twilight Zone. Our daily lives have been shaken, and upended. Death and disease are now part of our immediate reality. We must now mask our faces every time we step out of our homes. The world is in the grips of global PTSD. Which for many means, past fears that were thought to have been conquered and laid to rest, have been resurrected. For me, the fact I grew up poor, with a capital P, is once again infiltrating my thoughts. For those of you reading this, who also grew up poor, you'll understand what I'm about to share. I never ever pay the asking price for anything. I will search high and low for the best deal. I buy nothing without running whatever it is that I'm looking for, past everyone I know, in search of the best deal out there. If someone won't haggle with me? I'm not going to bother with them.

Not surprisingly, any decision about spending money sets off an inner conflict between myself, as a rational functioning adult, and you guessed it, that poor kid.   When Jill wanted to purchase the apartment next door to my small studio in New York, Oh, I fought that idea from the very beginning. First, if you've ever done, or thought about, any type of renovation to even a coat closet, in Manhattan, you might want to consider selling a body part! In very simple terms...IT AINT CHEAP! Then there was my argument that as a family, we spend relatively little time in the city. Primarily, it's where I stay when I'm working on the East Coast. That and our traditional Thanksgivings, so we can watch the parade live. I just could not rationalize why we would do this? But you know the saying, "Happy wife, Happy life." After more than a few delays, and a couple of "add ons'," purchasing the next-door apartment, along with the renovation's costs, doubled not only the size, but the value of our apartment, in one of the most desirable areas of Manhattan, New York. The apartment is stunning! The additional living space now allows us the gift of enjoying family time together in the greatest city in the world! Again, I was being that poor kid, afraid to spend the money. See that's the thing, it doesn't matter how much money you accumulate, the memory and fear of having little or next to nothing, never leaves you. Grow up! I'm embarrassing myself. We have two homes, one is a house in Santa Monica, California, and the other is our apartment in New York. People still come up to me and ask, "How did you know to invest in the two most desirable zip codes areas in the country? How did you see that?" I laugh and look at Jill. If it were just me, I'd still be living in my little studio apartment with my living room table made out of two cinder blocks and a wooden board table top with a roll of paper sitting on top! Yet, I've moved on. If you want to grow you must look and change. I did, even though I often stepped in my own way! I had changed my attitude toward money. Until now, the uncertainty of the world we find ourselves in, has scrambled the game board. Thank God, Jill's always there to help me understand (and remind me) my fear of waking up on the street, once again eating fried baloney with corn griddles and applesauce, is irrational. That I should not allow past memories restrict my reality. Intellectually, I know she's right, living small will keep me small! Emotionally? I'm still working on that!

I've never really had much confidence in the government. Watching how they've been handling everything now, has only shown me that I've been correct all along. This past year our government has proven to me, the majority of those charged with protecting the welfare of its citizens, have put their own self interests ahead of our country.

As for my own self confidence? I am the youngest of four siblings, two brothers and a sister. My mom worked as a waitress; my dad was an insurance clerk. This meant they really weren't around much. The times we were all together were great. However, money (rather the lack of it) was always a sub-current in our household. They always managed to keep us in the bare necessities. We'd get a pair of Chuck Taylor Converse sneakers but, of course ours had the swanky stitching, or the off-center tongue...the irregulars. Hey, the regular ones were way out of our meager budget! One time I was telling this "back in my day" story to Hallie and one of her girlfriends. I was making a point about something (which I've now forgotten) but I finished up with, "Everything was irregular." At which point, Pammy chimed, "Gee Mr. Collins, my mom takes a laxative every day. Maybe you should try that." TMI Pammy, TMI.

Anyway, my point being, self-confidence, was always two steps forward and one step back. I was athletic, friendly, and helpful to others. People said I was funny. Looking back, I see that I used humor as a way to find acceptance. I dressed differently from a lot of the other kids. Cuffed jeans, sweaters covering up holes in my shirts, irregular sneakers. I was shabby long before it became chic! I felt insecure in other ways too. Not having the money to go with the other kids, for something as simple as getting an ice cream, when the truck went through the neighborhood. I'd hear kids talk about going on vacation. We never went on vacation! Hell, we never even went to a restaurant for dinner. Vacation for us was a summer trip to Nanny's (my grandmother) house in Massachusetts. The fact that I was the only sibling allowed to stay with her through the entire summer, was teaching me to have confidence in myself. I'd cut the lawn, help out with household projects, like building a new wrap-around porch on their house. I learned to work in their big garden. I'd help get the ground ready, plant seeds, harvest the plants and then deliver tomatoes and lettuce to neighbors. Then I'd go to the local beach club to swim and play. It was heavenly!

I remember, at the beginning of one summer, I was playing on a Little League baseball team in New York. Being athletic, I made the All-Star team as the starting shortstop. Naw, no way was I hanging around for that. I was off to Nanny's house in Massachusetts for the summer! People were amazed that I chose not to participate in the All-Star game. It was easy. I disliked baseball! I found the game so boring. The pitcher stands out on a mound in the middle of the bases, pitches a ball then waits while he counts to a minimum of twenty-four seconds. He pitches another ball, picks up a small bag of rosin, claps it in his hands a few times, then drops it. He looks to the catcher for a signal, shakes his head no. He waits for another signal, nods in agreement, winds up, pitches ...and a Ball is called. I'd be on the bench snoring!

Starting as a Stand-Up comedian, you have to develop stage confidence (which is nothing more than displaying self-confidence in a space full of strangers) if you want to be successful. Have you ever heard about some comedian who was funny, but he/she just never found their voice? What that means is they never developed their confidence. It's taken me years to make what I do on stage appear natural and relaxed...confident. Believe me when I tell you, I've earned my spots performing, earned being asked to appear in special comedy events. I loved meeting the well-known comics, but many were aloof and would keep to themselves. I would go to a club, perform, gain some confidence, and then look for the next spot to perform. I wasn't in the comedy cliques. There were those times I felt left out when I wasn't asked to attend a party or a special occasion in the comedy world. I would stay home, honing my material, writing about what I found funny, and what I thought others would see as funny also. Many times, I would be up for a part in a movie or a television show and not get it. My self-confidence would take a hit. Immediately I'd wonder whether I was "good enough." I'd question myself, "Why not me? What was wrong with me?" What I now know, and am fully comfortable in saying is, I'm really good at my job! I do have the confidence in my abilities, in my talent. However, I've also come to the realization that in order to reach your highest level, you need more than talent...you need connections. My time with agents has always been short lived. I'd grow impatient, opting to just handle everything myself. I've never had the experience of having a really good agency in my corner long enough, to bring me to the attention of people in the position to keep me moving upwards. Have I made it harder for myself, to reach the level of success I thought I could obtain? Probably. But I've stayed strong and remained on the path I've chosen. Through it all I've persevered - because I knew I had something to offer! Besides, I was doing alright on my own. I did a few commercials (Certs, Speidel watches, Budweiser beer, and others.) Once you're seen in a successful one, they come looking for you! From those commercials, I was asked to host a television comedy showcase titled, VH1 Stand Up Spotlight. As my confidence continued to grow that poor kid would show up, once and awhile, whispering in my ear, "Am I good enough? Can I do this?" Nevertheless, I went on to get parts in movies (one with

Dustin Hoffman) and other stars. I pride myself with being a consummate professional. It doesn't matter if it's a commercial, movie, corporate job or a comedy club, I prepare. I add any new material right up front, gauge the audience, perform to my highest standard, then just as importantly...I enjoy myself!

As I've grown older, I find my day-to-day self-confidence on par with my professional confidence. I'm more self-aware in all circumstances and am willing to take hold of a conversation, add to a story or just be comfortable being quiet. People hold me in high regard and that's very flattering and humbling. At the end of the day, I've made peace with that poor kid from Queens. Because he's grown into a successful adult, fully capable of breaking down self- imposed barriers, both real and imaginary. For that, I thank God and my wife!

I feel as though having a special needs child has helped me break through the walls I'd built for myself. I don't want to have any walls around my girl Madison. I've fought to make sure that she has a life of love and understanding, freedom from stress, protected from the worries and hassles that I've had in my life. I find it hard at times when I'm home and there's no help with Maddy. The challenging times that I've experienced have reminded me that she was given to me to protect and love with a stress-free existence. God has given me the constant reminder that she's here for both of us. So, when the pressure builds in me, time to pull the plug and lighten up the situation; whether it be feeding Maddy, combing her hair, walking around the block, putting her shoes and socks back on when we're in the car, or screaming at the top of her lungs as we're walking the dog. It really makes you look at what's important in life!

JJ Walker

Sinbad

Chapter 9

OUR JUDICIAL SYSTEM:
WHERE RIGHT IS MIGHT...FOR A PRICE

●

A LAWYER WITH A BRIEFCASE CAN STEAL MORE
THAN A THOUSAND MEN WITH GUNS.
-Mario Puzo

I'm writing this now as a catharsis for my own repressed emotions. Having to be the example- when you really don't want to be! However, Right is Might, The truth will set you free!

The back story. I was involved in a lawsuit with a person who, twenty-two years ago approached me to record (tape) one of my Stand-up performances. I admit, I was impressed when he told me one of his clients was Richard Pryor. We came to and signed an agreement. He was to do the recording, sales and distribution, with both of us sharing in the profits.

After a year of making money – he asked to record two additional performances. I ask, "Don't we need an additional signed agreement, to cover these?" His response, "We don't need a signed agreement – we're doing well, let's call it a handshake deal." I guess my yearning to become a household name as a well-known comedian, as well as continued financial growth, overcame my practical, business side. Jill even mentioned, "Bobby, I don't trust this guy – he looks seedy to me. "After talking with other Comics, I learned I could get cassettes and CDs to sell at venues, at a third of the cost he was charging me. Originally, I was paying eight dollars, then he reduced it to six dollars. I found out I could get them for like a dollar fifty each! Ding Ding Ding - Red flag- Warning! Ok, so I figured I'd hire someone I know, to do the recordings of the two new performances.

So, I hired another guy to tape, edit, design a cover, and include liner notes as well as chaptering the performance on a CD. The problem was, I didn't know how to get the finished CDs distributed to the various markets. I went back to "Mr., Handshake" and told him, "Here are two CD's, complete. How much will it cost me, just to have you handle the distribution?" He said he would just deduct his cost from my royalties.

Low and behold my own naivety in not consulting an attorney or seeking out an alternative player to distribute my performances would come back to bite me!

A few years ago, I found myself wandering around in the age of the internet. This is not a place I find enjoyable, nor do I profess to understand it or possess the skills, or desire to master it. One day my daughter's casual remark, "Dad, you're a texttard." Would be pivotal to a detrimental discovery.

I hired a millennial to handle my social media in an effort to up my social networking bigtime, boost my popularity and to increase my fan base. I told him, "I'll give you a month, and then we'll see how you do, and we'll decide if we go forward." After two weeks he calls me, "Are you aware that your five CD's as well as your two DVDs are being sold on 12 different sites? Including Spotify, iTunes, Amazon etc." After looking into this, I found out the guy I had hired to record my performances, (five CDs in total) registered all my copyrights as his own! "Mr. Let's do a handshake," this Bottom Feeder... had been receiving money for years as the copyright owner of MY material. I was appalled! Despicable!

I called the Sound Exchange – the company that pays the artists, to figure out how this happened. I explained, "It's my understanding, as the Artist I am to receive 50 percent." Now, I was being informed, "No. The artist receives 45 percent, the copyright holder receives 50 percent, and their company (Sound Exchange) receives 5 percent." I reply, "How is it then, that I am only receiving 50 percent? I'm the artist AND the copyright owner!" There's a pause, then another person gets on the phone.

"Mr. Collins, I have to tell you we have had quite a few problems before, with the individual you are inquiring about. Let's say, you received as the Artist, $355 thousand (at 45 percent) then the purported copyright holder (at 50 percent) illegally received at least $400 hundred thousand." Our recommendation, "Consult with an Attorney."

So... to all my fellow comedians or should I say Circus people, let me share this cautionary tale. You work your whole life, establishing yourself as a successful comedian. Touring, writing, and honing your craft, all to see the laughter and love from the audience. Knowing, full well in your heart, at the end of the day it is all worthwhile! You learn quite a bit about yourself during the journey. Gratitude, for opportunities that find you. Selflessness, giving with no expectations. Priorities, God first, family second, career third. Finally, the big one, Honesty. Pretty simple. I do what I say I'll do and I expect you to do what you say you will do. And when other people who have MONEY as their God and do whatever it takes, lie, cheat and steal –

they need to be exposed for who they are! I went after "Mr. Handshake," by filing a lawsuit.

There are those who use the law, as a means to accomplish their ends. Because they know how "the system" works, they've done it so many times before. The time spent on depositions, putting together discovery, motion hearings, the filing fees, the attorney's fees, all to grind away one's resolve and bring people to the table to settle.

What I (we) went through, in order to serve witness to the manipulation of the LAW and how people use it for their own monetary gain (a whole business in itself) is an ordeal that should be avoided! Sad but true. "Mr. Handshake" and his attorneys, went as far as to freeze my wife's account, along with my special needs daughter's social security allowance bank account! Oh, they know how to manipulate the system and they will do whatever it takes to wear you down to the point of concession, in an effort to dispose of a lawsuit. Again, being raised believing, "Right Is Might" I did not back down. When I know I'm right then I must follow through with my conviction. Did this action pull me out of my world of laughter, love, and my comfort zone? Oh boy did it! They messed with my family, including our nonverbal, daughter with limited mobility. This has had an enormous effect upon us. We've been frustrated, angry, upset, and saddened. Coupled with all we hear from our attorney is, "It's going to cost you more money to continue." We have accepted the realization that even if/when we win, we will lose money. However, when you have a horse in the race, you see VERY clearly the people who know how to work the system for their own personal gain. It's so sad and disconcerting. These people with no conscience or heart, whose sole motivation is...Money! Sometimes I just want to scream HELP! But no one hears me. This whole debacle ripped me out of my world and pushed me into another. I know ...things happen for a reason. You handle it, follow through, and learn the lessons that come along with it. I will say, this type of event will open you up to take stock and move on. OK, so these are new lessons to learn, more mountains to climb. Like I said...things happen for a reason.

After many, many months we won the case and all my copyrights were restored back to me. Their financial settlement was ridiculously low. But, their prime objective was met – they received what they set out to get - MONEY. In summation (I learned a little legalese). I will now use an attorney for all future endeavors. I will look hard and deep into the person I'm dealing with. Furthermore, I will conduct myself in the same positive, strong, fearless and honest manner that has (for the most part) served me well. Minus a minor slip up here and there in the future.

Addendum (there's another one) in my group of basketball buddies (for the past 20 years we've had a weekly game) which is my only connection to most of them. One of the players is an attorney. He overhears me telling some of the other guys about "Mr. Handshake" and tells me, "Hey Bobby, I'll handle this guy for you. We can set it up as a contingency." I ask, "What does that mean?" He tells me, "I represent you, we file a lawsuit and I get one third of whatever we win. If we don't win, we're done." Well, that sounds like a plan to me. So, I hired him. After a few months he tells me, "This thing is more involved than I first thought. It's taking more time and costing me more money than I anticipated...waw, waw, waw." So, I give him some money (no small chunk of change either, and figure it'll motivate him to get this thing done and over. Then after one year of working on the case (and me periodically giving him money) in total, around $10,000, he contacts me. Again, he laments how my case is costing him more money and time than he can afford. That's also when I find out he screwed up some of the work he did on my case, and the Judge sanctioned me, to the total tune of $24,000. Finally, he states, "This case is simply costing me too much time and money to continue." I ask, "So you're done? Now what do I do?" He replies, "Get a new attorney. "

I hire a new attorney – the one who eventually wins the case. But "Basketball Attorney" the one who withdrew, makes his own play and comes back after me for what? MONEY! Not only that, he waited a year (until the statute ran out) to file suit against me for one third (his original contingency agreement) of the money I did receive! I tell him, "It was your decision to withdraw, you wanted out!" He reluctantly concedes, but then comes back with, "Seventeen Thousand Five Hundred dollars, and I walk away." Unfuckingbelievable! As if that's not enough, he goes on," It will cost you more to pay my attorney fees, than it cost for your attorney who won your case!

Do people like this really exist? Doesn't Karma play a role in this person's life? How does his wife, or his children view him? How do you explain that somewhere, sometime, something will happen in his life... that will not be good! A mutual friend of ours, who also happens to be an attorney and who has played basketball with us, is likewise appalled at his actions. He tells me, "He does not have a leg to stand on, I'll speak to him." He does talk with him, telling him what he's trying to do is wrong and to

82

NOT file his lawsuit for the one third, contingency amount.

Ah, they know the MONEY game and they know how to work it. "Basketball Attorney, also knew by waiting for the statute to run out, I would not be permitted to recover any of my costs, defending against his lawsuit. This is so sad but true. The lingering effect this has had on my wife, my children and myself, for that matter, is frightening!

Will I continue to fight the good fight and win? Yes, I will! Will I continue to be an example to myself and my family? To pay whatever it costs to expose this type of vile venom, wherever it manifests? You bet I will! Don't get me wrong, there are many fine, honest, and hardworking attorneys in the world. However, ... I now see, firsthand, how the court system can be manipulated by unscrupulous men and women for their own personal financial gain! People beware out there, these parasites exist.

Chazz Palminteri

Chapter 10

LIFE AT HOME DURING THE PANDEMIC

●

WHEN I USED TO WATCH THE TV SHOW TWILIGHT ZONE, I THOUGHT THAT

*KIND OF THING NEVER HAPPENED, AND NOW HERE I AM IN THE MIDDLE OF
ONE.*

-Bobby Collins

My Italian wife is wonderful, kind, giving, beautiful inside and out. She's thoughtful, caring, fun and creative. She is the most heartfelt person I know. However, when it comes to me being home for any extended time? Oh My God! Get me a rope, so I can hang myself! What is happening in this country? In the world! Every soul on the planet is hostage to A Global Pandemic. A pandemic, as defined by Wikipedia is, "an epidemic of an infectious disease that has spread across a large region, for instance multiple continents or worldwide, affecting a substantial number of people." My definition? A moment in time when the Universe "Bitch Slaps" the planet! Our lives have been upended. Every soul on the planet has been sent on a path, different from the one they were on one year ago. It is now, more important than ever, to do your research. Know the scientific facts about Covid 19. No more blind faith in politicians or... government. I grew up in New York City. Politicians were a joke. The way we saw it, a politician's job was to keep getting re-elected and build their own personal wealth.

Know the facts. Get the information for you and your family from doctors and scientists. People who have been educated to address the nightmare the world now finds itself. Not politicians! Our former POTUS suggested we drink bleach...household bleach! People...Use your own common sense! My wife uses disinfectants on everything, the counters, the floors, the cars, the toilets, the door handles...my groin area.

I found myself at the airport and I'd forgotten my mask. (It's a learning process.) Everyone had a mask on, I did not. A lady (wearing her mask) in line beside me, starts rummaging through her purse. She pulls out a Kotex pad and a rubber band. Handing them both to me she says, "It's kind of a filter." I wore it- it worked. Common sense. Wear a mask, don't touch your eyes, your nose, or your mouth, and wash your hands. I went to pee - I used my elbows – it was not steady. When we first encountered this virus, everyone was freaking out! For who knows why, everyone was loading up on toilet paper. Hoarding it by the pallet! Does Charmin cure Coronavirus? Priorities are balancing out. Wiping our butts is no longer the end all! Get all the facts from qualified intelligent people and look out for your family as to the best action to take. I do like the social distancing though. In life we all know people whether that be family members or friends, who've taken a turn and are not nice people to know anymore. "Hey...HEY! Too close, 6 feet, 6!" Problem solved.

Thanks to the pandemic, my wife and I are together 24/7, Love you pookie, it's becoming undeniably evident, Jill and I are getting older. I can't pick up Maddy so easily, my basketball knees play a castanet solo every time I walk. Ole! I have no less than three pairs of (cheater) glasses in my pocket at all times. Long about the middle of last March, Jill, my best friend, mother of my children, woke up one morning, looked over at me and demanded, "How much toilet paper can one man use? Seriously - are you wrapping your entire arm!" As I was telling her," Honey, I just want to be thorough." She cooed, "Good morning, my handsome lover boy," followed by, "Bobby, have you noticed...do you think that maybe, maybe, I have mood swings?" Immediately (and a little frightened) I answered, "No. No! I certainly have not honey." I love you so much! Without skipping a beat, she shot back, "And another thing. You never put the toilet seat down. WHY!" I mumble, "I don't want to pee on the seat!" Just like that - menopause gathered her portable fans, ice packs, Black Cohosh...and moved in. For those of you who don't know what menopause is, it's a medical term meaning... "RUN!" Its evil seeps into one's house and gets on the furniture, the walls and drapes. Grab your Blacklight flashlight, see for yourself!

It's inevitable, as we age, things change – sex changes. One morning, Jill's watching me as I get out the shower, after about a minute she says, "Bobby, you used to have a nice bubble butt. Now it looks like Mitch McConnell's chin." Unruffled I replied, "Sometimes I have to lift my cheeks in order to wipe." The other night we gave each other the look – you know that look. We hop into bed, I get on top of her, she screams out, "My back my back!" No problem, I say, "I'll flip, you get on top," two seconds into this, I grab my leg yelling," Jill, my leg – sciatica, my leg!" Now we lie in the same bed, each on our own side, separate pillows and gurgle at each other, "Hungry? Grab your fan - I'll get my glasses - and let's go to the kitchen for a bite."

I'm starting to think the magical mystery tour may have just begun!

After 911, my (then) nine-year-old daughter, after listening to the news, looked at me with such uncertainty and sadness in her eyes, a look I will never forget and asked me, "Daddy are we going to die?" Instantly, I replied, "No we are not. We are going to live, love, and laugh like we always have!" Now here we are, in a world pandemic, and my twenty-nine-year-old daughter is looking at me with those same eyes, her lip slightly quivering, and asks me, "Dad, are we going to die from this virus?" Just as quickly as I did in 2011, I responded, "No we're not! We're going to be safe, we're going to wash our hands, get the most qualified information from the scientific experts. We're going to learn from our mistakes, push the reset button and move forward. We're going to learn a person's character is what matters." Times are truly changing! We all must be proactive in setting the example. To raise all of us up to be what we can be, to help each other achieve kindness, equality and tolerance. I'm hearing and seeing too much disharmony. People have so much unwarranted anger, anxiety, and stress. Do not let fear and panic, map out the future. We will get through this!

Now back to my wife! I understand that as we age, both of us are going to go through changes, both physical and mental. I do realize that part of reaching healthy maturity is being able to change past behaviors to the benefit of those around you. Having said that, I find comfort in knowing my everyday behavior is of no real consequence to anyone in the world, except...my WIFE.

This whole drama with this pandemic has really made me look at myself. Never in my forty-year career, have I spent this much time with my family. My not getting on planes traveling to get to the next gig has been enlightening. Seeing the look on the face of my special needs daughter, Maddy, because her dad is here, every day, laughing, playing and cuddling is (as Donald Trump reiterated constantly) "tremendous!" At the other end of this "home dad" experience, I find myself wishing I could run and hide from the millennial one. She lost her job a few months back, so now she's working for me, building up my "social presence." It's something the tech savvy crowd (young people) spend a lot of time using. Facebook, snap chat, twitter, knick knack, paddy whack, give a dog a bone...all are part of this new toolbox necessary to keep a good comic connected and relevant. By the end of our first "work" day... I can tell you one hundred percent, why she lost her job! I can hear some of you saying, "Oh Bobby, she's young, she'll find her niche." No, no she won't. I know by saying this, there will be some parents who will be upset. I can hear them now, "You know that's a mean thing to say about your child, and I doubt very much if it's true." Oh, it's true.

By the end of the first "work" day, with her personality and humor it was a good fit! Thank God because I see in her friends, and kids that age. They have no "hustle" skills at all. I remember back when I'd be selling clothing in the Garment Center, or constantly schmoozing to build up my jewelry customers. I was out there every day hustling to make money, so I could work the comedy clubs at night (for free) pursuing my dream to stand on a stage and see people laugh.

Another thing. All this pandemic togetherness has resulted in my getting a little snappy with the wife. To be clear, I (along with almost everyone in the entertainment world) have not worked since last March! For us, there is zero bacon to bring home! We still have families to support, people who rely on us. This job, my job of stand-up comedy, has always been somewhat irregular. I do my own bookings, which in itself is a full-time job! Before the pandemic, I had established a system. For a certain number of days, I would be out on the road performing (anywhere in the country) then for a certain number of days, I would spend time home. It was a good system! Now, everything is blown to shit! There are no places to perform. No one knows when venues will reopen, but to be sure, it will be a whole new ballgame! For one thing, masks. For performers, and specifically comedians, so much of what we do on stage, is geared by how an audience reacts. Reading an audience will be strange, when two thirds of everyone's face is covered! Even the sounds of laughter will be muffled. Right now, it's anyone's guess how long our population will be required to wear masks, in the public sectors. When venues are finally allowed to open...will anyone even want to go out for a night of laughter? Even given the uncertainties of just how the future for entertainers will shake out, I cannot tell you how much I miss being in front of an audience, making everyone laugh! In the meantime, I'm trying to write new material. I'm not sure where to even begin. This surreal world where we find ourselves, surrounded by disease, death and economic upheaval doesn't lend itself to "funny!" Which is why I've turned to writing (and finishing) this book. An undertaking that will (hopefully) help to loosen and exercise my comedy muscles. Here's what I think. We're all experiencing "Shell Shock," to various degrees. You hear everyone talking about getting back to normal. Forget normal. Normal was a time before. We just need to get back to a place of functionality. Return to living unencumbered from constant concern for our own health and safety as well as our loved ones. We'll get there, but we are indeed witnessing the resurgence of a whole new (hopefully better) world! Thankfully, throughout this whole isolation time, the phone has rung constantly, with friends and family checking in to see how we're doing. The internet is burning up with fans around the country touching base and venues are beginning to reach out with dates for this coming summer and into the fall. I love it! However, there remains a small pocket of emptiness inside of me that I will have to fill myself. On stage. Making and hearing people laugh. Okay now that I got that out... I have to vacuum the upstairs (boss's orders). Even though a surgical staff could operate off our floors – she has them so clean!

I try not to watch television news because of all the devastation and death tallies. This is the time for the strong to rise up and be the examples. To be better than we think we are – to help each other, comfort and aid each other. It's time to show the true character of who we are! Sure, I wake up thinking about money, bills, work, writing, my family, and health. But then I settle down and thank God for the blessings he's given me. Allowing me to get out there (granted, to a smaller circle) to do the best I can for myself, my family and anyone else who needs it – that's who we are! To combat those moments of fear, uncertainty and doubt, I've had to learn to enjoy the stillness, to practice gratefulness, and offer daily thanks for what I have. You see those people, who upon self-reflection, do not like what they see. Yet they remain unwilling to change. Those are the people I worry about!

I was out walking to the beach with my wife and my daughter Madison. Most people along the way were kind and observing correct social distancing. Some however, were not so thoughtful. Despite the fact they could see me pushing my special needs child in a wheelchair, they made no effort whatsoever to establish social distancing. I was the one to cross to the other side of the street or walk down the street until they passed. As we were walking, I was eating some peanuts and one got caught in my throat and quickly started to choke. Just as quickly I managed to cough it up. A guy walking his dog, about nine feet away from us, screamed out, "Hey! Watch with the coughing, cover your month! What the hell's the matter with you?" We all stopped and looked at this person, who was quite visibly overreacting, due to his fear of virus contamination. Using my most calming voice, I explained, "I had a peanut caught in my throat, I just needed to clear it out." He was not hearing any of it. He was rambling on, "Can't even take a walk...people spewing whenever, no consider...blah blah blah. Being the kind person I am, I instructed him, "Shut The Fuck Up!" Sometimes people have to hear it in a way they'll understand. He didn't say another word, just quickly walked away. Jill looked at me and said, "Boy - you really handled that well."

Just the other day Jill and I stopped at a red light. We watched as a man walking his dog, drinking a cup of coffee, started to cross the street in front of us. The light changed, but the man was not yet to the other side. As we sat there waiting, he turned to face our car and started screaming at us. The radio was on, so we couldn't make out what he was saying. I gave him a yeah yeah, head bob and very nicely waved him on to finish crossing. He stops dead in the street, raises his cup and douses our windshield with coffee! Then as if nothing had happened... he keeps walking towards the curb. Jill and I just sat there for a second in silence. "Hmmph," was all we could come up with. People are just snapping left and right! The constant anxiety everyone is feeling is causing us to change how we're interacting and communicating with other people. We must remain civil towards others, we are all dealing with loss, of one kind or another. For some, they have lost loved ones, others their livelihood. We are all castaways in a sea of uncertainty. Now is the time to take a deep breath, get recentered, and together we will come out the other side. We will get through this just like we're gotten through many other things!

Being home these last few months, I've learned a lot about family and it's been wonderful! Of course, I'll be joking about it on the stage saying things like, "Statistics show an increase in domestic violence. Oddly enough, the number of male mouth breathers has decreased."

I've learned to help out like never before, doing the dishes, walking the dog three times a day and making up the beds. I now know the correct way to set a table – forks on the outside–knives inside, closest to the plate and on top of the napkin. I've mastered the garbage. I can confidently separate regular from recyclable. All of this while donning rubber gloves and a properly fitted mask. That's just working around the house.

Leaving the bubble of your home also requires PPE as well as subjecting yourself to impromptu body cavity searches. I went to the hardware store, a man at the door rolled, what looked like a cooking gadget, across my forehead, then squawked, "Ninety-seven. You're good, go on in." I stopped by the drugstore; they were giving everyone a colonoscopy at the entrance. What's next, rhinoplasty to get into the flower shop!

To keep my millennial "assistant" busy, she and I have been making short videos. Silly stuff of me putting on costumes, acting out the changes we're all having to make during this pandemic. Everything from wearing a gorilla mask (covers your mouth and nose while it keeps people 6 feet away). Playing "Can't touch this" while I get down with some interpretive dance moves. I've been filmed doing chores around the house, wearing a scuba mask and flippers. We've Zoomed, how I'm coping with having no haircuts, no workouts (pick-up basketball) and no restaurant dining.

I have to say, Hallie and I had a lot of fun! Just goofing around, letting people know it's okay to laugh, and hopefully to show laughter IS the best medicine. What I found surprising? The amount of people who watched and the number of calls I received from people asking me, "Mr. Collins, would you be interested in doing a Zoom performance with some of your fellow Comics? I respectfully tell them, "I've seen comics perform, alone, in front of a camera. I credit them for what they're trying to do, but...without a live audience, those performances are missing something. They always come off flat. Thank you for your interest." I have caught a few of these Zooms, truthfully, I would not want to do one myself! Then there are podcasts. I watched a few, Comics questioning each other about how and where they started, where they are from and where do they live now... yak yak yak. Many people watch or listen to them and find them fun and interesting. No disrespect, to me they're boring. What I think would be fun is to sit around in the Green room with some comedian buddies, like we all did before everyone got benched. A bunch of wing nuts, bullshitting and goofing around, making each other laugh over road stories, then share that with viewers. Yes, I'd do that. Well guess what? I just finished taping ten episodes of Bobby's Viral Friends. While we couldn't be together physically, I got to sit at home and "visit" my comic friends, Ray Romano, Jay Leno, Tim Allen, George Wallace and Colin Quin, in their homes. We had a blast! Talking about how we're holding up, laughing, sharing road stories, laughing, about everything...as if we actually were in a Green Room. The people who have seen the rough cuts, loved them, and appreciated being "the fly on the wall!" We'll see where it goes. It was a reminder for me to keep an open mind. (Especially when there's no money coming in!) To take some creative risks. You just never know what direction the world of entertainment is going to be heading.

As a performer my job is always to lighten the mood. Since this pandemic, the chances to do so (professionally) have been slim to none. Sure, I can sit with friends on the front lawn, six feet apart, laughing, finding the fun in the situation. A pretty woman passes by, gives us a friendly wave, and I throw out, "Sorry lady, I'm married!" We all share in a laugh, and for that moment forget to be vigilant of one another. I'm not even going to talk about the people who react to my remarks as if I'd just punched a puppy or kicked a cat. Which is why I look for more receptive souls within my community of confinement. I'm still a New York guy at heart, who finds joy in entertaining! I do take advantage of my ability to read an audience when the situation presents itself.

Every Wednesday, here in Santa Monica, there's an area that holds a Farmers Market where people can set up booths and sell their fresh produce. I've known the people there for years from my weekly trips to get fresh flowers (Jill loves flowers.) Since California has implemented strict "corona shopping restrictions" the lines at the farmers market are now huge. A couple of weeks ago I was getting ready to make my flower run. Only this Wednesday, I came downstairs wearing a red jacket, and a lanyard hanging from my neck, attached are two badges that I've held onto for years. One is from The Grand Ole Opry, in Nashville, Tennessee, and the other was my high school photo, that was used at my fiftieth-class reunion. Jill's at the bottom of the steps, looks at me and asks, "What are you doing?" I tell her, "There will be over 250 people standing in line to get into the farmers market today. I will not be one of them. I (flicking my hanging cards) have credentials, to get through security! The market opens at 8 am - I get there at 7:37. Wearing my mask and gloves, I walk to the front of the line, as I'm casually tucking my "credentials" into my red jacket (which coincidentally looks just like the city's security jackets.) I get to the head guard, tell him, "They sent me down here to just check-up on how procedures are working out." We talk for a few minutes, I comment on the weather, then about how crazy it is now that everyone has to wait in lines. We share a laugh, as I say, "Keep up the good work," and walk directly into the market. All people want is to be validated. To be spoken to with civility and acknowledgement that we're all in this horror show together. I've now done this for ten weeks in a row... every time, he waves me through.

Another time, Jill asks if I could go with her to Costco to pick up household supplies. (She's got a list longer than my car). We arrived not long after they opened at 8 am. The parking lot is full, there's got to be, and I'm not kidding, about three to four hundred people standing in line with shopping carts. Everyone is separated six feet apart winding through the parking lot. Plus, there's a long separate line for the sixty-five and over crowd, as well as essential workers, including doctors, nurses, and medical staff. Jill sees the line and says, "Let's get out of here, I'll come back another time." I say, "No wait. Just follow me and wait by the pole at the front of the line!" Wearing my mask and gloves, I head towards a security employee, controlling the front of the line. I get close enough to read the name on the front of his shirt, it's Don. "Hey Donny," I holler out. I can tell he's trying to figure out if he knows who just called his name. I lift up my mask and give him a big smile, "Donny, how come your hair looks so good?" He gets a big grin as he tells me "I did it myself." I laugh and tell him, "My wife tried cutting mine, but I ended up looking like Gumby!" This makes him laugh, and I add, "Come on, cut mine." We're looking at each other like we've known each other since we were kids. I give him a head bob towards the front of the line, meaning...can we go in? He looks at me a minute, then asks, "Are you alone?" I quickly answer, "My wife is right there, waiting with a gun to shoot me." This gets a big smile as he says, "Come on in!" With that we're in and out of Costco in less than thirty minutes! Like I said, all people need is to be treated respectfully, shown some acknowledgement and share in some humor. As we're leaving the parking lot Jill looks at me and says, "I can't believe you. You do this all the time." Like I keep telling her, "It's a gift!" She still thinks I'm a total asshole. However, we've been to Costco three times since then, and Donny lets us right in! HELLO!

Being at home during this pandemic has made me realize – I have been living in another world – a world where I'm most comfortable. I have never before had to deal with an insured shipment of 'lost' books, which were sent to, what is now, a closed tour venue. I call the post office; they tell me they were delivered. I fill out forms. I know the people at the venue, so I give them a call. They tell me they never got any notice of a delivery, or ever received the box of books. I call the post office back, tell them what the venue told me. They give me a tracking number, about the length of Einstein's theory of relativity, and tell me to download and fill out another form. Then the post office informed me that the books were returned to the sending address in California. Now a month and a half later, I got an envelope from the post office. Inside I find the cover of the box which was used to send the books, along with a note. The note informs me, the shipment was separated/damaged from this package. They offer their apologies and inform me all lost items are sent to their mail recovery center, at the post office. I suit up in my PPE and go down to the Post office and speak to two people there. One guy's lips fell off with, "Can I help you?" The other keeps complaining, "I can't understand what you're saying, your mask, I can't understand you." I ask for a supervisor, he tells me I have to download a different form, fill that out and send it in. I told him I tried, online, for two hours. I could tell he was having a party in his head not inviting anyone. He confirmed this with, "Yeah, we're really backed up. Keep trying." So, the books are still MIA. But good news. When I got back home, I found a Christmas card from 2017, in our mailbox.

Now my wife asked me to call up Spectrum, which provides our phone service, as well as TV and internet, to straighten out connection issues. Originally, our provider was Verizon, which became Frontier. Then we started to have some problems with the connections, which were Wi-Fi speed, and the television picture quality. So, we switched everything to Spectrum. The cost was about the same, but they claimed to have higher internet speed, with more efficient service. Talk about misinformation! Seems Spectrum consists of two different entities - business and residential. One side is completely separate from the other. When you call for service, it's a matter of either or. I explained I would need three(residential) lines for the house (TV, internet and phone) and two (phone and fax) for my office(business). The installation guy shows up to set up the boxes for the TV and internet. He tells me he can't split between residential and business. I told him that I explained what (how) I needed the lines when I talked with your rep the phone. The installation guy says, "Sorry whoever told you that was mistaken." Long story short, terrible business platform, misinformation...plus they charged me twice for switching everything over to business! It doesn't end here. For the last two months, I have received two bills (for one business platform) I paid the lesser one, then called them to explain, "I originally wanted residential and business, however after being told they could not be split (at one address) I had everything put under ONE business account. STOP sending me two bills for one service!" This call may be recorded or monitored for customer satisfaction...Honestly, no one knows shit or offers any type of help to actually remedy the situation. I will tell you this, after talking with this guy, the Post Office looks like a model of efficiency!

Next, my adventure with California's DMV Department of Mother Vuckers ...oh my God! We have four cars. The car I drive gets hit when a guy backs out of a driveway and rams into my back door. The door's totally crushed, but the car's drivable. I take it down to my mechanic and he tells me, "Best scenario here is to declare the car totaled and have the insurance company pay you the value of the car." So that's what I do. Insurance pays me four thousand for a car I purchased a couple of years ago for forty-five hundred. Great! I'm from New York City, everyone's door is bashed in, besides, my car drives fine. Unbeknownst to me, once a car is declared totaled, you then have to go to the Department of Mother Vuckers (let the games begin.) The car has to be registered again. Three Hundred and Fifty-Six dollars. Once a car is registered salvage, it has to be issued new license plates. Seventy-Five dollars. There's a little burp in the back light, so I have to take it to a light and brake specialist before I can take it to be inspected. So, after I get a new back light, One Hundred and Eighty-Six dollars, it passes inspection. Total, Five Hundred and Seventeen dollars; two hundred new gray hairs, and endless hours I'll never get back. This is what people deal with on a daily basis ON TOP of a pandemic? Thank God I'm a performer! Post office, Spectrum and the DMV...there's a reason I don't own a gun! Once I'm back out on the road working, I just might stay out there forever.

Some observations about what's being shoveled at TV audiences (having watched more TV this past year, than I have in my whole life.) Hollywood stories about this one getting a divorce, that one getting new lips. My favorites? Celebrities, sitting around their pools (bigger than my apartment in New York) outside their mega mansions, wearing some cutesy mask, reminding us to wash our hands and that we're all in this (pandemic) together. NO we're not! No one I know is "riding it out" in their second home, somewhere in Caribbean.

With thousands of people leaving this world daily, why should anyone care if the red carpet will return soon? I know for sure; this is not a top priority to the medical community. The Housewives of Dumb are canceled, so now they're playing reruns. Like you want to watch these train wrecks again! People seem to be wising up. I think David Frost had it right, "Television in an invention that permits you to be entertained in your living room, by people you wouldn't have in your home." Like I've said, "We are better than this!"

DID I OR DIDN'T I?

As we're learning more about this virus as time goes on, some sources have suggested that this coronavirus was in California far earlier than anyone knew and could have been here as early as December 2019.

Which is why I'm sharing this. The second weekend of January 2020, I was sick as a dog. I awoke in the middle of the night, sweating to the point of being able to wring out my tee shirt. It was so bad, Jill slept in another room for four nights. Hey, traveling by air all the time, I get sore throats, aches and pains. I'll give my doctor friend Alan a call and he'll prescribe some antibiotics for me. The next day I'm up and good to go.

Not this time. I laid around the house for four days, Jill was keeping her distance, bringing and serving me food from a tray. Always being that tough Italian, screaming, "It's the flu, you'll be alright in a few days!" This was different, my whole body was in pain. Ever the professional, come Thursday I boarded a night flight to Denver. Friday morning, I woke up early, to go do television and radio promotions. I put on my best face, but I was not well. I got through the appearances, then went straight back to the hotel and got into bed. I felt terrible. I stayed there until just before I left to go do two sold-out shows. Waiting in the green room with the opening act, I needed to excuse myself, so I could go cough in the bathroom. Even on stage, I'd get a hunk of phlegm and need to turn around and swallow quickly, so as not to disrupt the flow of material. When I was done, I immediately went back to the hotel, and stayed there the entire next day. The next night, I felt a tad improved. I kept thinking. Who ever said the show must go on? I've had the flu before, but I kept telling Jill, "This is different." I finished my shows, returned home where I fully recovered. Back then, no one knew anything about some strange virus that would eventually turn into a worldwide Pandemic. No one was testing for it. But I know what I experienced was NOT a normal flu!

I've spoken to a fellow Comic who, along with his girlfriend, currently has COVID-19. They both described the same symptoms that I had the week of January, 2020. The fever, sweating, the tremendous aches and pains throughout the body and that constant coughing up phlegm. It's been eight days for them and they feel fine, with the exception of a persistent, nagging cough. People who have low immune systems or have a tendency to pick up these ailments, stay safe and secure!

Jay Leno

Bobby

Family

Chapter 11

MADISON – MY INSPIRATIONAL SPECIAL ANGEL

•

PARENTS OF CHILDREN WITH SPECIAL NEEDS CREATE THEIR OWN WORLD OF
HAPPINESS AND BELIEVE IN THINGS THAT OTHERS CANNOT YET SEE.
                                                                                -Anonymous

Sometimes I get these thoughts. Wait, that sounds like what you'd say to a shrink. Messages? Nope, I'm not writing the Old Testament. Information - that works. From time to time, I get information, from who the hell knows where, or why. I've learned to just go along with it, it'll fit in somewhere, sometime.

One morning I woke up and asked Jill. "How's Maddy's eyesight doing?" Jill, being the most hands on mom I could imagine, tells me how she takes Maddy every year to see the eye doctor to check on her eyes. I have learned raising a non-communicative special needs child, who is low functioning, has had multiple back operations, self- stimulates by shaking her head and rolling her eyes back can be challenging. So, when I get information coming to me questioning her eyesight, I stop and act on it right away.

I call her eye doctor and make an appointment. I go with Maddy, we sit, and I hold her hands while the doctor examines her eyes and places drops in them. It is a struggle as Maddy tries to pull away, but after about twenty minutes and a Six Hundred Dollar bill (they don't take insurance) the doctor informs me that her eyesight is getting a little better every year. Bull shit! My information tells me otherwise. I come home and ask some doctor friends for the names and locations for the best eye doctors in town! I get the number of a world-renowned Eye Institute, right here in Los Angeles. I get a name; I make an appointment and take Maddy there. The doctor takes us inside his office and examines Maddy's eyes, then he asks, "What have her other eye doctors told you?" I reply, "They tell me her eyesight has been improving as she's getting older." He frowns before informing me the most prominent doctor in the field of vision, from Saudi Arabia, happens to be at Children's Hospital in Los Angeles. I ask, "Can you get us an appointment?" He says he'll check. When he returns, he tells me, "Unfortunately, he's already returned to Saudi Arabia but his assistant from China, Dr. Reiser is still here. I've set up an appointment for you to see her today." Together we head out on our mission to get the best possible eye care for this beautiful young lady. We arrived at the Optometry Department of Children's Hospital Los Angeles. After a lengthy wait, the doctor comes in with at least 7 doctors in tow (keep in mind – it's a teaching hospital.) She takes Maddy in for an examination for about an hour. "What have her other doctors told you?" she asks me. Again, I answer, "That as she's getting older her eyesight is getting better." Dr. Reiser, who wears glasses herself, tells me, "Mr. Collins, when I take off my glasses to go to bed – I can't see a thing and I'm a minus seven. Your daughter Maddy is a minus fourteen. I'd be surprised if she's ever seen your faces."

I felt as if someone just punched me in the stomach. So many thoughts were passing through my head. How come we were getting such wrong information? Who can you rely on? I flashed back to my waking up and asking Jill about Maddy's eyesight. Where did that come from! After seeing the confusion, disappointment and sadness in my eyes she tells me, "I have a procedure that can correct your daughter's vision - however it is old and isn't done anymore". I tell her, "Go back in and do it!" She tells me, "You'll have to go through your insurance company and chances are they won't approve it." I plead with her to go back in and do the procedure now, "I'll pay cash!" She tells me she can't.

I come home, call my insurance company and they confirm. That method is not done anymore; that if it were done and if by chance, the doctor was to scratch Maddy's eye, she could be blind for life. I shout to the voice at the other end, "What do you think she is now? If it can help, even a little... let's do it!" The insurance company says no. I call my attorney and have him send a letter informing the insurance company they are being sued! Weeks pass and I stay in touch with Dr Reiser. About a month later, as I'm coming out of the cleaners in New York I receive a phone call from Blue Shield. I answer, "Funny you should call. I'm in New York City, just coming out of my attorney's office (little white lies don't count). An unamused voice says, "I find no humor in that. Are you some kind of comedian?" I tell them, "Yes and I perform all over the country. Just imagine the type of publicity I can provide for you." They said they'd call me back. In ten minutes I received a call from the insurance company informing me they were allowing the eye procedure to proceed. God works in mysterious ways!

It takes another month to get everything set up. Finally, we take Maddy in for the procedure with Dr. Reiser and her crew. She tells me she's looking to get like - 25 % sight back. I tell her, "I'd be happy with 10%!" As is our tradition (we have a lot of experience with hospitals and procedures) I dress in scrubs and stay at Maddy's bedside, until she is totally under and unconscious, then she is wheeled away. Jill and I and her sister wait and wait, for what feels like an eternity. In reality, the procedure took about an hour and a half. Dr. Reiser emerges to give us a report...with tears in her eyes. I felt my heart sink, I managed to choke out, "It didn't work." Dr. Reiser regains her composure and tells us, "I didn't get 25% or the 50% I'd hoped for... we got 100%! Maddy can see perfectly. Her eyes well up again, "This is why I became a doctor, for the moments like this!" All four of us stand together crying to beat the band, as we all declare, "Maddy can see!" We take Maddy home with these safety harnesses on her arms so that she can't touch her eyes through the night. The harness needs to remain on until tomorrow, when we have to go back to the hospital to have the bandages removed from her eyes. When we get home, we feed her, love her, and offer her comfort. Here's the catcher. She gets up on her feet, her arms harnessed at her side, bandages covering her eyes and proceeds to trail around the house, like it was nothing! Which in her reality - nothing had changed (apart from the harness, which really didn't seem to bother her). Because in fact, she had been maneuvering her surroundings blind for years! The next day as Jill and I are getting ready to take Maddy to get her bandages removed, Jill catches me blow drying my hair and putting on nice clothes. She stops and stares at me "What are you doing?" I happily reply, "Well, if she's never seen her father...I want to look nice for her!" "Jill snorts (with a smile) "You're an asshole!"

We take Maddy into the hospital, they remove her bandages and Doctor Reiser tells us to be calm and to keep in mind...she's never seen your faces. Maddy looks at us, hears our voices then pulls her face close to mine and starts to cry loudly. What a moment! For the first time she was able to associate our voices with a face. Unbelievable. Thank you, God! Listen when information comes in – act on it – it's coming in for a reason! Follow your instincts. I did.

Jill and I have had talks regarding Madison's future. Do we place her in a group home with other special needs people? Are we doing everything we can as parents to allow her to grow into a productive functioning adult? Are we hurting her by keeping her with us? Do we hire people to assist Maddy in her everyday life? Can we afford that? Ahh the questions! I've called and inquired in different areas of the country about the programs for special needs adults. It's like the middle ages. There are three year waits for these people. I've visited programs from Pennsylvania to Florida and have seen the different situations available for these special people. It's sad. The unfortunate truth is, most of society treats those with special needs as second-class citizens, rather than the gifts to society that they are! We should care for and protect them. Help, provide for, and nurture them. We need to celebrate their lives and serve as an example of the type of caring society, we should be. Am I being too altruistic and naïve? I was always brought up that a nation is as strong as its weakest link, we should set the example for ourselves and the rest of the world with the poor, the homeless, the mentally ill. We are the example! After seeing these group homes and don't get me wrong some are fine, we've decided that Madison is best with us! She's low functioning, she's used to her home, her room, her "work program" every day. Again, the questions arise, what do we do with Maddy as we continue to get older? Is it fair to expect her older sister to care for Maddy, while creating her own life? What about Jill and Bobby's world? Will we be able to retire to a life of traveling, will we be in a position to drop things at a moment's notice to move to a different part of the country? These and more, are all things we have to consider. Thank God I chose the right woman to partner with to help make these decisions!

According to statistics, seventy four percent of parents with special needs children divorce. Is it hard? Yes, it is. Is it rewarding? Yes, it is! When God gives you such a gift it is indeed a blessing! God does not hand out these angels just to anybody. I'm honored! I am fully aware I'm not in this alone. I've been blessed with a woman who not only embraces the blessing, who finds and radiates joy in "All things Maddy!" My calls home from the road are answered by (a sometimes exhausted, yet always invigorated) my holding down the home front, full of love - spouse! What can I say, I love her! As for me, I'm that Comic traveling from city to city making people laugh and knowing full well the love I have for my daughter whom God entrusted me with is an inspiration! An honor! I must be pretty special if God gave her to me!

Madison has always been an inspiration to me. To see my daughter who has gone through so much in her short lifetime is truly humbling. I'll be on the road performing, get back to the hotel and look at her pictures. Tears well up, smiling, I whisper, "Thank you God." The sheer strength of this child, to not only survive, but to instill such joy into our hearts is overpowering.

To state it simply, Madison was born bent over. It has taken a series of three major back surgeries, and many procedures (she has thirty-two metal screws attached to two large metal rods in her back) to get her, more or less, straightened. Me? I lie around on my back for a while, and I get shooting pains just trying to sit back up. I cannot imagine what she has endured!

On one check-up visit to LA's Children's Hospital, through x-rays, it was discovered that one of the metal rods had broken and would require another open back surgery. My heart sank. Not only for my beautiful child, but I now have to steel Jill, as she gets off the elevator, with the news. The pain in her eyes was equally heartbreaking. Another time, I took Maddy into the outpatient part of the hospital, to find out why she was now developing seizures. The decision was made to run an EKG test. As they attached the wires and monitors needed, they administered Chloral Hydrate, to try and help keep her calm. After everything was in place, Maddy and I were left alone in the room. Maddy starts gasping for air and going in and out of consciousness - this is not right – I'm looking around for a nurse, a doctor...anyone to help her! I'm the only one there. I rip off the wires, and leads, unplug the monitors, swoop Maddy up in my arms and make a beak for my car. We're flying down the highway close to One Hundred miles per hour, racing to her pediatrician (a doctor I know and trust). As I quickly explained what had happened, the doctor took one look, quickly loaded up a syringe, and gave Maddy a dose of something. Almost instantly, her breathing normalized... she was okay. The doctor did tell me, "It's a good thing you grabbed her and got the hell out of there. Because of Maddy's physiological makeup, the use of sedatives is a tricky business." All I could answer was, "Thank you God!" I interpreted the information correctly.

Madison will forever have the mind, emotions, and frustrations of a toddler - in the body of a growing, developing young woman. Even though she doesn't speak (she has a repertoire of sounds to let us know Exactly what she likes, and dislikes...hair brushing!) Her mobility is limited. But she delights in rollin' through the neighborhood in her (dad powered) Jogger. She needs continual care/assistance with everything. She also needs to feel the sun on her face, feel/smell the salt air on a walk along the beach as well as the excitement and laughter brought on spotting a bird in the park! Appropriately timed naps are equally important with sensory overload. The days are long, tiresome, LOUD and messy. There is no growing out of a "phase." Are you ready? Here we go.

A day in the life...

First thing is getting her up and fed, getting her on and off the toilet (and wiped.) Next comes dressing her, followed up with hair brushing... cover your ears (people on the street hear her - and run) lastly brushing her teeth before heading downstairs to eat. After breakfast, pack up her juice, banana and yogurt along with her two ice packs to keep everything cold. Double check that she has her ID card AND her bus card (for the occasional times she uses the provided bus to return home). Next is helping navigate her out the door and into the car, hopefully with both shoes still on her feet. Fifteen-minute drive to her work program. Once there, it's checking that she still has on both shoes, exiting the car and the journey into the building. There's no goodbye kiss. She's gone until Jill or I pick her up at 3:00 p.m. Then we walk the dog around the block, before we get in the car to run errands. This is when Maddy lets it be known, she would prefer going to bed, over errands.

I feel I should take a minute to try and explain a few things. Jill and I do not profess to be "The Experts" on raising a special needs human. (Although, I think we (and I mean Jill) do a pretty damn good job!) Talk with any parent of a special needs child and they will agree, what can sometimes be perceived as "being mean" with your child is in fact, reinforcing structure, learning boundaries, and building self-confidence. Would it be easier to come home and allow her to go to bed? Probably. However, it would be a disservice. We want our children (both our children) to accomplish all that they can, with what they are given. An important part of Madison's wellbeing relies on structure and personal interactions. Which is why we have her enrolled in the day "work program." It's an important part of nurturing. Okay...back to rest of our day.

We finish up our errands, come back home, get dressed and go out to dinner. We keep it local, some place close by, where the people there know us and genuinely appreciate Maddy. After dinner, we take a short drive through our Santa Monica neighborhood before heading home. Once there, it's time to shower, toilet, pajamas, brush teeth, and pin up her hair. Every night, she and I play a game of hide and seek in her room. The game continues until she gives me THAT smile! A quick kiss and into bed! The last thing I say is, "Goodnight sweetie. I Love You!"

Now you have a realistic idea of what it's like in one day with a special needs angel.

A couple finishing thoughts. Finding aides to help us make our daughter's daily life (as well as our own) as "normal" as possible, while keeping her both physically safe and mentally stimulated ...has had its hits and misses!

It takes a truly giving, loving soul to care for special needs individuals. Once you find the one... do me a favor, pay them well! As much as you can comfortably afford. This person will spend as much time with your child as you do. They can be trained to meet the constantly increasing physical demands. They can be taught required emergency first aid procedures. However, it is difficult to find someone with the unselfish, caring heart required to find the joy and love supplied by such sweet, innocent souls. They should be worth more than someone who cuts your lawn or vacuums your house. They are helping raise your child!

I recall one Big Miss in this department. So much so, I became physically ill after walking into our house to find Maddy sitting at the table with snot dripping from her nose and her aide sitting, texting and talking on her phone. In the words of the current head Cheeto...You're Fired! It may take some time, but eventually you'll find the right aid for your child.

Jill, Maddy and Bobby

Bobby and his Angel

Family

Chapter 12
HEAVEN ZERO – BOBBY TWO

●

When I grew up in Queens, New York, religion was not much of a factor. In our family my mother, who grew up in the South (Shreveport Louisiana) was really the Catholic matriarch in our family. We kids very rarely accompanied her to church. The times I would attend, I was more interested in the calisthenics. Sit, stand, kneel - with a sit sit here and a kneel stand there, eieio. All choreographed with swirling smoke and Latin. I just always thought of organized religion as more of a socializing exercise. Churches were where neighbors could mingle after services. The religion practiced by a particular neighborhood was their common bond. That bond, for our neighborhood was Catholicism. Everything (practically everything) was centered around the church. The schools, the festivals, the Parish...the people. On those occasions I would make my way to church, I remember listening to sermons, and thinking, who doesn't know it's wrong to murder someone? I assumed everyone was being raised to know at least the basic stuff.

So, while we identified as Catholic, we weren't as they say, "practicing" Catholics. As such we attended public schools, then supplemented our perceived lacking in overall education, by attending weekly Catechism classes (to protect our souls). Every Wednesday, we would be let out of our school to travel to the local Catholic school to receive our religious instruction. Even though we were dismissed early on Wednesdays, there was barely enough time to beat feet to one of our buddies' homes (closest to the church) to read what we would have heard had we actually been in church the previous week. We'd quickly read through the passage, or verse, or whatever then give it a once out loud practice, so when/if we were asked to provide an answer, we could at least (hopefully) sound like we had actually attended Sunday Mass.

My first memory of entering that Catholic school has never left me. Public schools had their problems. There were student fights now and then. Some students would get caught smoking in the bathrooms. For the most part, especially when compared to our current world, we were just bad ass legends in our own minds. Walking through those Catholic hallways, to get to our designated classroom, took on an almost surreal atmosphere. What? Don't forget...I get information. Each passing room with an open door became a view master to another dimension. I looked into one room and saw uniformed students with lightly glazed over eyes, as they watched a ninety-seven-year-old nun admonish a 4-foot girl for the plight of the "pagan babies," until she cried. THEN she hit this little girl across the knuckles, with a wooden rod...for crying!

We get to our assigned room, and need to wait until the bell rings, and the class is dismissed before we can go in. A few of us move to just inside the door and off to the side. What happened next was unbelievable! A priest, the teacher, is beating on a male student. When I say beating, I mean beating...with a rod! (I'm sensing a theme) This assault act was happening right beside me. As he concludes his display of discipline, he looks over at me and starts to lean over, like he was getting ready to snatch me up. That's when I loudly said, "If you lay a hand on me, I will beat the shit out of you!" He takes a pause and walks away.

Forward to the present. Look at what's going on in the Catholic Church. Every day, more and more of these "men of the cloth" these "servants of God" are being exposed (and finally) being held accountable for their years and years of diddling young boys. I've known guys who would relate the most tragic stories of their own childhood abuse by priests.

Is it any wonder I'm a firm "Pass" on organized religion? Nope not on my top one hundred list. I've always known, deep in my heart of hearts, there were answers to, "Why are we here? What is our purpose?" I believe there is a higher power in the Universe. This power goes by many names, God, Allah, Buddha, etc. People use different names and practices to get to know the Creator.

I used to spend summers in Massachusetts with my grandmother, Nanny. She was a truly devout Catholic, and sometimes I would pray with her. She would explain to me, after our customary prayers, the questions she posed to God and what answers she would receive. She would relate something that had happened and how that was an example of the presence of God. It was clear that she knew the difference between the ritual of religion, and the meaning of the lessons. When I would ask her about (what I considered the basic bullshit part of the religion) she would explain that the church was there to provide people with structure in their lives.

For the holidays, our whole family would drive from the city to visit Nanny's true New England style home. It was very pretty clear who her favorite was. Every Thanksgiving she would always make me my own pumpkin pie. She was the one who always had my back, who stood up for me. Sleeping in her big, wonderful house was not without its challenges. Being the youngest, it was not easy for me to find my way to the bathroom alone, in the dark. Which is why my brother, Roy was assigned the task to walk me to the bathroom at night, should the need arise. One night during a Christmas visit, my brother refused to walk me to the bathroom. Instead telling me, "Just pee in the closet, no one will know." So that's what I did. The next morning, my Aunt Rena made a shocking discovery. I had peed all over the Christmas presents she had hidden in that closet! Nanny was the one who ended all the shouting and blaming with, "Bobby is just a little boy. Shame on you Roy. It was your responsibility to walk him to the bathroom. This is more your fault than his." Yes, I was very close to and loved my grandmother so much. I miss you Nanny.

I love my own family more than anything in life. But honestly, having two daughters and a hardnosed Italian wife, is no easy walk in the park! We roll with whatever ups and downs life brings to our door with a fun-loving, positive, and understanding way. Like anyone else, it can be hard at times, but we all climb the mountain together with a sense of humor. Hey, I'm a Comic for God's sake! My oldest daughter Hallie is a sensitive, somewhat naïve, and manipulative spoiled young lady. There are times when my growing up poor attitude pops up. I make comments that reflect the fact that I didn't grow up in Santa Monica, California, with children of famous, privileged White Hollywood types. Is there a part of me that wishes I had been brought up with that golden ring? NOPE.

My friend's fathers were shoe repair guys, truck drivers, department store employees, and an occasional bottom-feeder lawyer. These were your hard working, grind it out, day to day guys. I've learned it doesn't matter where you were brought up. More importantly it's how. To learn from those experiences, good and bad, then apply the lesson to guide and enrich your own life's journey.

A good friend of mine owns and operates many hotels throughout the United States. He's a New England guy coming from Maine. He's down to earth, wears his heart on his sleeve (pretty good basketball player). He's a good husband and father. Hallie would work summers at one of his Main hotels. She loved working there. She was meeting good people, making new friends, not saving any money to go back to college with but it was a great life experience for her.

Every summer, our daughter Maddy, attends her special needs camp in Vermont. Traditionally, we will use this time to visit our friends and check in with Hallie in Maine. We love New England! Plus, I've always enjoyed working there. Ever since that first year Maddy attended camp, the jaunt to New England is something we all look forward to.

Well, here it comes….. A couple of years ago, on one of our New England trips my friend Alan, and his wife, who we often vacation with, came with us. On the second day after our arrival, we decided to visit the famous Acadia National Park, where Cadillac Mountain is located. A spectacular mountain! It's the highest point on the east coast in the United States. I drive up the mountain, park near the top and Alan, Colleen, Jill, Hallie and I walk the rest of the way up. The view is breathtaking…unbelievably picturesque! You can see islands in the distance, as well as whale watching boats. The viewing area had ropes placed in an effort to keep the viewers at a safe distance from the edge. Since there was still a reasonable amount of space from the ropes to the actual edge, many people had gone beyond the ropes and were taking pictures (minus the visually distracting rope). Hallie ducks under the rope and takes a selfie I never thought I'd use that term. The resulting picture looks great! I ask her to take a picture of me, with that magnificent background. I slip under the rope and get into position. Hallie holds up her phone. For a split second, I get a Nano spin of dizziness and fall backwards! Now I'm tumbling down the face of the mountain. I'm knocked out immediately when I crack my head on a protruding rock. I continue to bounce boulder to boulder until a large rock, about fifty feet down, miraculously, halts my decent. Another foot to the left or right of that large blocking rock and I would have continued to fall another two hundred feet and died! I'm lying there on the rocks unconscious, Jill is totally freaking out. Hallie is hysterically crying and my friend Alan, who's a doctor, is climbing down to check my vitals. Colleen takes off to find a ranger. Luckily, there were a couple rangers nearby and they made quick calls to both a helicopter and an ambulance. It was determined that the helicopter would take too long to get to where I was. So, the decision was made (for the now group of rangers) to carry me up on a stretcher, to the waiting ambulance. Jill later told me, as I was being loaded into the ambulance, Alan was crying and telling the paramedics, "It doesn't look good at all."

I find myself surrounded by blinding bright lights. I remember trying to focus on where, and what I was seeing. It's my grandmother Nanny! She's smiling and walking towards, she looks wonderful, exactly like she did when she left me twenty years earlier. She gives me the biggest hug. Loving it I say, "Nanny, I missed you so much!" She smiles back, "Oh I miss you too! Do you know how much I love you?" I'm so happy! She pulls me towards her for another hug, telling me, "Bobby, you have to go back, you have much more to do. It's not your time yet." I respond, "Nanny, NO! I want to stay here with you." She's starting to fade away as she says, "No, you have to go back." As she disappears completely, I barely hear her say, "I love you!"

I wake up in an ambulance, with people leaning over my face. Jill is there, screaming, "Bobby - Bobby - Bobby - Bobby!" I open my eyes and with a very faint voice say to her, "I was just with Nanny." Jill with a controlled, yet a bit frightened tone, replies, "Bobby! You tell Nanny to go away. Go away!" I respond, "You can't talk that way to Nanny." As I begin to drift off again, I can hear the ambulance attendants talking about how they've heard of this type of "visitation" story before.

When we arrive at the hospital, I'm immediately whisked into a whirlwind of - tests, neck braces, needles, blood drawing, more tests, x-rays, monitors, cat scans and endless questioning by the attending staff. This might be a good time to let you know. I hate hospitals. I have always hated them. I'm not stupid, I do realize there are times they are necessary. They're just not for me. After about three hours into this, I lean over and whisper to Jill, "I don't want to stay in the hospital at all." The list of injuries begin: Severe concussion, contusions and bruising over face and body, several broken ribs. All in all, the staff and I are pretty amazed ribs are the only broken parts. No broken neck, legs, arms or nose/face. The Doctor comes in and says, "Mr. Collins, we'd like you to stay with us in the hospital for a few days - just to make sure." I quickly respond, "No thanks Doc. I have to keep moving, I'll be good back at the hotel." I'm helped up to dress, then I'm back at the Hotel ten minutes later. Jill and Hallie help me get into bed and tuck in. I hurt all over, even my hair hurts, and somehow, I manage to fall asleep. I'll be fine. Later that night I woke shivering, almost convulsing, rattling with cold. This was the delayed response of my body going into shock. I was freezing. Jill spent most of the rest of the night heating me with her hair blower. That hot air was heaven. The next day, I drove six hours to get to our apartment in New York City... to heal.

I'm here to tell you. This event was the most traumatic thing that has ever happened to me in my life. To reflect on how close I came to losing my wife and my two beautiful angels...was sobering. I was brought up to climb life's mountains, not fall off then. I'm still here...climbing!

Not too long after this, while still in New York, an accountant friend of mine, Jeff called and asked if I was going to be around the next day. "I am," I answered. "Great," he went on, "How'd you like to join me on my fly out tomorrow, to Block Island (an Island off the coast of Long Island) for lunch." I gave him a quick, "Sure! Where should we meet?" I met him at the Long Island train station, along with one of his financial friends, Alan, who was joining us. It was a quick trip to the Long Island airstrip (where Jeff keeps his plane) to board his plane and fly over to Block Island. The island is ordinarily a ferry commute to a summer fun destination. There are places to eat and swim with family and friends. It's a great place to get out of the hot, crowded city for "a day away," it's just a fun spot to hang out! Long Island people are good people, friendly, smart and know how to have a good time. We had lunch, laughed, watched a little volleyball on the beach with some really good players, it was an enjoyable afternoon!

We were mid-air on our return to Long Island, when Jeff asks me, "You want to fly the plane?" I said sure. I'm moving the plane up and down, looking out the window, watching the changing landscape of the ocean and land masses below. Simply beautiful and quite exciting. Jeff is sitting next to me. I notice he's starting to frantically check switches and gauges. Next, he tells me, "Switch back. I need to be back in my seat." We quickly switch back, and he tells me, "Hold onto the wheel, I need to check something. Reading the concern on his face, along with the growing lump in my throat, I ask, "What's going on?" He informs us, "The indicators show the landing gear is not working. The wheels are not going down." He tries to hand pump them but to no avail. He does a turn to make a slow pass over the airport. He radios the small Long Island airport and asks for a "visual check." He completes that pass. They radio him back, "Visual check confirmed. Your landing gear did not engage. You have no wheels down!" With that he circles back towards the airport, in order to bring the plane down. This time I can see fire trucks foaming the airstrip – a small wave of terror runs through my body. I look back at Alan, who has become the palest human being I've ever seen in my life. He's practically translucent. Since I'm in the front passenger seat, Jeff tells me, "The second we hit the ground I want you to open your door, then immediately roll out and tumble onto the airstrip." I give him my are you nuts look, "No way! I didn't die falling off a mountain three months ago, and I'm certainly not going to kill myself now "rolling" out of this plane!" It was rough and bumpy, but we landed successfully. The firemen came over to check on us, asking if we were okay. In unison we convincingly chimed, "We're fine." As we're walking towards the terminal, Jeff asks us, "Uh guys, I'd really appreciate you're not mentioning anything about this... to my wife."

Riding the train back from Long Island to my apartment in Manhattan, I had a chance to do a mind review of the two potentially life-threatening events, which had occurred disturbingly close together. A calming inner resolve came over me. Bobby, in the past two months, you have stared death squarely in the eye, and walked away, twice. Apparently, my dear Nanny was right. I still have things to do in this life. I am not finished. Thank you, God. The journey continues...

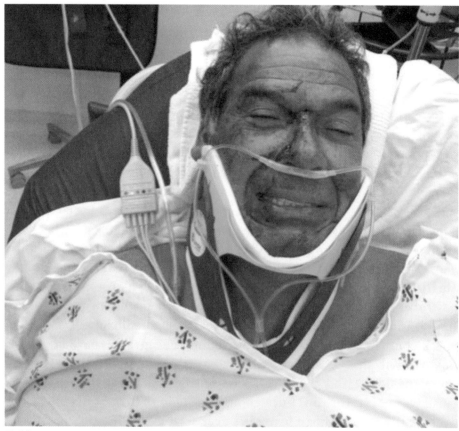

Bobby

Bobby with pilot Jeff Gilbert

Regis Philbin

Bobby with Christopher Plummer and Jill

Chapter 13

IS THERE A DOCTOR IN THE HOUSE?

●

I'VE BEEN POKED AND PRODDED IN PLACES I'D ALWAYS PRIDED MYSELF ON KEEPING UNTOUCHED FOR THAT ONE SPECIAL DOCTOR WHO GIVES ME A RING AND A PROMISE.

-Libba Bray

Growing up in Queens, New York, my best friend was Alan, a guy I needed to remind, "Alan, are you aware...your socks are pink?" Turns out he was colorblind! He still is, and we're still friends! Actually, we're practically neighbors, here in California, where he's a renowned doctor, specializing in spinal surgery. Occasionally we get together to do a men's shopping spree. He likes the way I dress, so I just get him the things that I would wear. He's a wonderful guy and probably the most astute person I know.

When I stop over at his office, I see how he treats his patients with such care and thoughtfulness. I can easily understand why people line up to come see him. He has a caring bedside manner. He is a doctor who listens to patients – hears them and discusses options they could be taking. That's the kind of doctor people want and need. There have been many doctors I've noticed while growing up, with the attitude, "My shit don't stink," or "I'm a DOCTOR... what do you do?" Nah, not for me. I always like the real quality of a person, no matter what they do for a living.

I've always looked at how our society views doctors, as if they're gods. They wear the white jackets with a stethoscope hanging around their necks - they can do no wrong. They have the skills, training and education to heal us. Society holds doctors up to a higher status. Call it intuition or a spiritual signal, I have always felt that doctors treat the symptoms, while we create the causes of our own ailments. Don't get me wrong, we need doctors. However, if we really look hard at ourselves, we can many times see what we're doing to our own bodies to cause sickness and pain. I've always believed that!

There have been times when I knew I pushed too hard, traveling, eating, performing and not exercising. Times I would not understand what I needed to do, to address some physical issue I'd be having. I thought, it's always good to be sure! Alan knows how I travel to perform, to make people laugh. He knows I'm exposed to different parts of the country, and people, that I live on the road, in planes and hotels. He would always warn me to take care of myself - mind, body and soul. Keep your mind working with ideas, your thoughts positive and sharp, your family concerns paramount. Heal thyself, take the time out to exercise, stay in shape, work on what your body is screaming at you to work on and take care of it. Follow your spiritual path, your inner feelings and talk to your God for advice, understanding and guidance to follow your path, to see where you're coming from and where you're going. Take the time to see there's a bigger picture in your world and ask for help for you to conquer all obstacles placed in your path. I do.

Sorry, back to my friend Alan. In case you missed it, I will occasionally have a party in my head and jump away to follow its course...but I'll always invite you to come along! My doctor friend Alan knows my life as the court jester who travels from castle to castle making the minions laugh and then moves on. I just love my life! He tells me that if I ever get sick, no matter where I am in this country, to call him first. Ding, ding, ding! What's up? He then goes on to tell me that there are many doctors out there practicing medicine for the wrong reasons. Wow! I ask, "In your opinion...give me a percentage" Ready? He says, "About 40%!" Did you hear me? About 40% of doctors out there, do it for all the wrong reasons. Ego, money, status (the country club) money, acceptance, money, rather than being called to help heal. The country is now realizing the devastation of the thousands of prescriptions written, for opioids. Written, many times by doctors in cahoots with the pharmaceutical industry. While they were filling their coffers, this country was building towards a full-blown opioid epidemic. Sad but true.

So, I'm working on the road and I develop a cough combined with a scratchy sore throat. I have to perform and I'm not feeling well at all. I stop into an urgent care facility, fill out a form, see a doctor, get an examination and wait for some tests to come back. While waiting, I call my friend, Doctor Alan. I tell him where I am, what's going on and that I'm waiting on some test results. He asks, "Bobby, can you put the doctor on the phone?" I ask the doctor, "Would you mind talking with my best friend, who is also a doctor?" He agrees and takes the phone, he's convivial, and I think, How nice, I'm getting a second option. Isn't that what we really all want – bring in a few more opinions and we can all sit and decipher the results? The urgent care doctor smiles and hands me the phone, "Your friend wants to speak to you," and he walks away. I get on the phone and Doctor Alan says, and I quote, "Leave now and get out of there quickly, he doesn't know what he's talking about." I leave, telling the doctor I have to run, but I will come back in a little while. Wow! So let that be a lesson for me. Always ask for a second opinion. Not every doctor is trustworthy, knowledgeable, or honest. (Remember those 40%?) …. Saved again!

There was a Saturday night, after a show, when I drove from a theater in Boston, instead of staying at a hotel there, to my New York apartment. I figured it's only a four-hour drive, and I rather sleep in my own bed… you always feel more comfortable waking up in your own bed! I did the drive, arrived at my apartment in New York and unbeknownst to me, my beautiful wife Jill, had flown in earlier that day from California, and was already in bed asleep – a pleasant surprise! I cuddle in and I go into a coma from the ride and the show. I wake up being tapped on my shoulder while someone is saying, "Bobby, Bobby!" I look up, Jill's standing over me holding my underwear with a pair of tongs asking, "Bobby, is this your underwear?" I say, "No." She says, "You're the only man in the house." I cave, "OK, they're mine. She asks, "What happened – these are disgusting, they look like a crime scene!" I say, "Nothing happened, I drove home from Boston last night, and I stopped off and got some Chipotle." Jill continues, "No more tidy whiteys for you. From now on… you have to wear black underwear!

Fast forward, back home in California, Doctor Alan is over to the house for dinner, when he asks. "Bobby, when's the last time you had a physical?" I reply, "Never, I've never had a physical. I'm good… in good shape, I work out, I feel good!" He goes on "Bobby, I know how you feel about doctors treating the symptoms and how we create the causes, yet you still should have a physical." Jill chimes in, "Tell him Alan, I tell him all the time!" Laughing I say, "She only wants me to get a physical, so she knows if I'm about to die, and she gets all the money!" She responds "YES!" The next day Jill and I are sitting in Alan's office, waiting for me to take a physical. I thought it was going to be, open mouth, breathe, hit the knee, hit the chest, turn your head and cough. No, it wasn't. I had to run a while on a treadmill, get x-rays, run some more, stretch. I finish, go back to his office, Jill and are sitting there when he comes in with my chart and states, "Bobby, you're in great shape, but I will also need a fecal sample, a urine sample and a semen sample." My wife jumps in and says, "Just take his underwear!"

I usually go to a doctor for a specific ailment, like a sore throat or a breathing problem (wheezing). I show up, fill out the forms, see the doctor, get a prescription, go to CVS, fill it and I'm finished. I generally take the pills for a few days and stop after my ailment is gone or almost gone (I know, that's not what you're supposed to do.) I must say though, I'm not a pill guy. I'm at the age when conversations with friends seem to be more and more about doctors. (If you're my age you get it. If you're young... wait.)

Which is why this is where I'm at. It makes sense to have A Master Doctor. An elite internist of whom most doctors have heard of, or they know is well regarded and respected in his field. I get the name of such a doctor, make an appointment and go see him. I give him records of my past health issues, pictures, MRIs, and cognitive reports. I'm reminded that he does not take insurance and I will have to pay for the consultation. He goes over everything from my past with me, from shoulder surgery, to allergies, to my fall from a mountain in Maine, to sore throats and knee bursitis, as well as some vestibular(balance) issues. He looks at how I was treated, what was done on my behalf and he then discusses with me the steps to be taken going forward. He'll hook me up with the best doctors in every specialty from cardiology, neurology, urology, neuro – ophthalmology, allergic – rhinosinusitis, amongst others. Most of these doctors do not take Medicare but some do – let the games begin! He gives me the name of the doctors; I make the appointments. My best investment is Me. Stop with the money thing, pay if you must, but make the commitment and just do it. Side note, I wouldn't think twice about paying cash if it was for my wife or the kids but me …. Medi what?

Ok, I make seven appointments with seven doctors within a week. Why? Because I can! A neuro-ophthalmologist, to check the eyes for present and future expectations. A neurologist to consider future balance and post vestibulopathy resulting from falls from mountains and basketball playing. A podiatrist, for knee and foot injuries resulting from years of wear and tear on the body. An allergy-rhinosinusitis for the breathing and sinus infections, constantly picked up, from being in different parts of the country (allergens), picking up bacteria from planes, and just performing in front of a lot of people. A cardiovascular consultation, i.e., stress test, to check the heart. A urologist to find out... why I'm peeing as I'm typing this right now! A vitamin and supplement doctor to maintain the notion of "a body in motion continues to stay in motion." And no, Jill doesn't want to hear any more about all of all my aches and ailments. So, I go to the medical corporation and allow them to work their money- ego-magic to make sure I can continue to be the Doctor of Comedy.

I have all the results of my "medical marathon" sent to The Master Doctor, so that he and I can compare all the information and then determine the direction we want to take for the future. As for the other doctors, they don't want to be found incompetent by the master and lose their status. It's like having checks and balances, so I'm getting the best service for my money. In the past, when you visited one doctor, they felt as if they had to give you something even if there was nothing wrong – a prescription, a referral, a future appointment. People keep in mind, it's a business! It's not like when we were kids and a doctor in a white coat, spent time with you, and genuinely had your best interests at heart. Now, the days of single practitioners are gone. Doctors today are corporations, who find their attention and time, sadly, more focused on the bottom line (money) more than your wellbeing. It's up to you to keep an eye on YOU! I've said I always felt doctors treat the symptoms and we create the causes. Don't get me wrong, we need them, but keep your eye on the donut not the hole. You are the donut!

I'm basically going through the doctor palooza to check on my aging health, and more importantly, to see if I am having actual health issues, or just responding to getting older. I go see the first doctor and, of course, I mention the Master Doctor who recommended this doctor. He looks at me and asks me how I know this doctor. I tell him he's a friend of the family. I was very aware that he was being so professional and so thorough, dotting the i's and crossing the t's. Doing tests over just to be sure, advising me and explaining to me the different consequences which can occur from not testing for this or that. I left the office feeling like I was just given the best medical consultation I had ever experienced. He takes neither Medicare nor my back up secondary insurance. Welcome to this money game.

I just completed a medical procedure called a Urolift. It's a clipping up of your prostate to control the constant urinating at night! So now I won't need to get up to pee six times a night. I can return the porta-potty I keep by the side of my bed! I got to the surgery center at six-thirty in the morning, signed two hundred forms, before being taken to the back to get settled in. At eight-thirty, I'm met by the doctor and put out by the anesthesiologist...let the games begin! I wake up an hour later – time to go home! Done – I'll pee blood for a day or two and get addicted to oxycodone for a few days, then hopefully I'll be fine! Ahh, Bette Davis was right, "Old age ain't for sissies!"

I'm told to get some vaccinations I've never had. There are so many, but he tells me to start with three, Hepatitis, Shingrix, and Pneumovax 23. I agree and the nice girl in his office tells me to go to CVS to get them, as it would be so much cheaper! I ask what the price would be to get them here, in the office, and she tells me five hundred dollars! Hello CVS! I called the CVS pharmacy and made an appointment to get the three vaccines, which will cost me one hundred and thirty-five dollars.

I show up at CVS, pay, and sit in a small side office while they inject me with the three vaccines – one in the left arm, two in the right. Within two hours of arriving home I can't lift my right arm up at all and the pain is excruciating! Couple that with some tingling in my right hand and a fever that has me changing my t-shirt six times throughout the night! No sleep, sopping wet, accompanied with chills so strong. that Jill grabs a blow dryer, sets it on high and uses it all over my body to try and warm me up! The next morning, I wake up and my right arm is racked with pain. I have to go see my doctor the next morning for a blood test for my cholesterol. I arrive and inform them of my pain, and they can't believe CVS did all three vaccines at once. And they're asking me, who told you to go to CVS? I didn't want to get the girl in trouble, so I told them I just assumed it was OK to get all three vaccines! It's been three days and finally I can feel the pain leaving my body – but it was hell! People be careful and don't look just to save money like I did.

Chapter 14

FRIENDS: THE GOOD, THE BAD & THE UGLY

●

MANY PEOPLE WILL WALK IN AND OUT OF YOUR LIFE, BUT ONLY TRUE

FRIENDS
WILL LEAVE FOOTPRINTS IN YOUR HEART.

-Eleanor Roosevelt

I'm sure you've known people who just want to be friends so they can say you're friends. In Los Angeles, there are people who want to be friends to see what they can get from you. I find that so sad and selfish. Remember friends for friend's sake? Those times of fun, joy, and laughter. Having someone you can reach out to for an honest opinion or help with a problem. The simple ease and genuine appreciation of a valued friendship. I have a few of those and it heals my heart when we talk and get together. I have old friends from high school, as well as college, who pop back into my life every once in a while. Sometimes these encounters can be bittersweet. Stories of your shared past can evoke some painful memories or bouts of unbridled laughter... or both. One thing for certain, these "blasts from the past" allow you to evaluate how friends have changed (or not) and where their paths have led them.

One old high school friend went on to achieve incredible wealth by selling his company for one hundred million dollars! OMG what I could do with that kind of money! Full time 24/7 care for Maddy, extended family trips, financially support other special needs families. I learned he's never married (trust issues) and has numerous health issues. He does have a girlfriend, but it's clear that the relationship is lopsided. There's no equality in respect or love for that matter. It is obvious and sad, at least to me, that he's paying a high price for a relationship that will never work out. I don't judge, yet I truly don't like to be around them.

Another friend is a chiropractor up in Lake Tahoe, CA, (God's Country). Ever since Jill and I moved to California, thirty years ago, I've made it a practice to secure Tahoe gigs, at least once a year. That way, I can make money while the two of us get to enjoy some time together in beautiful surroundings, have some fun skiing, and throw in some fantasy hotel sex - just kidding! Truth is, we just love getting away to Lake Tahoe!

So much so that when we were discussing where to spend our honeymoon, I suggested, "What about Fiji, or Hawaii? Or maybe Europe?" Without pause she answered, "Why don't we go skiing up in Tahoe?" DONE. Just another example of why she's My One!

Where was I going? Oh yes, my college friend in Lake Tahoe has fallen on hard times. His brother, a medical doctor, also lives up there. They don't speak to one another anymore. It has something to do with the parents passing and leaving a home in Florida to them. One brother didn't want to sell, while the other wanted to sell for the money, blah, blah, blah.

The problem, as I see it, is my friend does not know how to promote his chiropractic business and is unable to develop a financially stable practice. He has moved his office and treatment space into his home. Let me tell you...that's attractive! He is living month to month. He is always asking people, who can do something for him, for their help. For example, he will impose on others in town, at a casino, a restaurant or a nice hotel, for referrals to his practice. I was with him once when he introduced me to someone who knew who I was, that I was a stand-up comic. This person had stopped coming to him for whatever reason, so my friend was playing me up and the fact we were friends, with the sole intention of getting him back as a patient. So awkward and embarrassing!

Then there was the time I arrived in Tahoe a day or so before Jill. My friend knows that when I'm working at the casino, I get a stipend for food. On those times when I get in earlier than Jill, I will take him out to various restaurants. He loves it and usually, I don't mind, it feels like the old college days when whoever has the money pays. What bothers me is how he simply takes it for granted that I will pick up the tab when we go out. On top of that he also expects to go eat when HE wants. He never even considers the fact that I need to plan my meals around when I have shows to perform. One time I asked him to drive me three miles to the Dollar Store. I needed to pick up some toiletries. He made it clear he considered this an inconvenience - a hassle. My way of thinking is you help people whether they are going through hard times or not. We learn early about being kind and giving to a friend with no expectations of receiving something back. You give to help out. But you will find there those in your life who settle in and become very comfortable being a Taker. While we were eating one night, I became a little annoyed with his self-appointed role as the taker in our friendship. This was going to be a tad tricky. I casually mentioned to him, "Do you ever think maybe you're being a little selfish with your expectations of those around you? Have you considered looking for someone to help you navigate through life with? You know someone you can rely on and someone to rely on you." His response, "I have my dog." Alright...a swing and a miss. I quickly change the topic and move on.

Another good friend of mine is a very successful doctor. He's never married but lives with a lady in his big house. He never speaks about her or their relationship at all. He always greets my special needs daughter with such love and warmth. However, I can read the sadness in his eyes, when the two of them are interacting. I've always wondered why he never had a family; he'd be the best father I know! It's a topic I've never brought up, not my business. I have noticed whenever I ask, "So how's Kerry?" He gives me a quick, "She's good." That's it. I don't push for more, but I can't help feeling we're both getting shortchanged in our friendship. I believe solid, true friendships are when you both recognize you have one life to live, so live it to the fullest. Friends are the people who will join you joyfully, as you discover who you are in the world. Someone who will share each other's laughter and fun. To ride out the triumphs as well as the tragedies...together.

I can remember a time, hanging with my friends, when we could talk about everything. Like, "What's going on with that hottie you're seeing? Is it good? Is there a future? What's she like? How's her family? Did you meet them?" Now, I'm finding some friends give me the sense there's been this invisible boundary imposed. Any effort on my part, to try and get friends to open up about what's going on with them, is curtly dismissed. To be honest, this makes me feel uncomfortable. I'm discovering I really don't want to be around people where I can't be open, express myself and hopefully help to make things right. That's friendship! Aside from my increasing uncomfortableness, I just hate seeing the sadness this particular friend is trying to hide.

My best friend is Alan, I've known since we were both ten years old. I'd pull him aside in grammar school in Queens, New York, to tell him he was wearing pink socks. He was color blind! We both live in California now, not far from each other. We speak almost every day; we laugh about our families and our wives. We're all best friends. I'm godparent to his kids and he to mine! You know when you feel so comfortable when you're together, it's your extended family. He introduces me to his friends, and you can see the admiration they have for him, not only as a locally prominent doctor, but as a human being. I kiddingly try to dispel that image every chance I get!

Alan grew up just as poor as I did. You can sometimes catch that commonality when we're together. We'll give each other that look, which takes us right back to being those poor kids, who couldn't afford to go do most of what the other kids with money did. We talk about it, laugh about it, but we never forget about it! I love Alan from the bottom of my heart! Is he awkward? Yes. Do food particles collect in the corners of his mouth and lips while he continues to talk? Yes. Are people continually pointing out, "Uh Alan, you've got something there on your lips." All the time! There are times when he'll start whining about his perceived money problems. I give him that look - which he knows means - shut up! That's when I remind him, "You have money, a beautiful home, a rental property, great kids – one becoming a doctor, the other working on her law degree." Stop complaining!

I'm circus people. I'm the one who should be complaining! I'm the one who is running around the country like a court jester going from village to village making people laugh. Working, looking to make the money, and now, "Here we go! We're doing it!" Damn, I wish I'd grown up rich. Nah, I'm just saying that because I too, can get caught up with that money thing! We have to be happy with who we are. Of course, we can change some things we don't like about ourselves. Yet we are who we are for a reason! Did I just say that?

I recently received a phone call from an old college friend checking up on me and the family during this pandemic. It was nice catching up on old times, laughing, being twenty again! He shares that he's now working at a company in Brooklyn, New York, with another one of our old friends. He goes on to tell me this other friend, whom we both have known for thirty years, screwed him and other people in the company over money! I learned, the two still work at the same company, but have not spoken a word to each other in months. Here's the Irony of this. I parted ways five years earlier, with this same person! He had tried to use his money to pull off a power move on me. Are you kidding me! Where the hell did you grow up? Argentina? I never received an apology. Hey, we all do the occasional overstep, but we catch ourselves. We apologize, do a humble reach out and we all move on! I thought he would see the error of his ways in a few days, suck it up and call me. Thought maybe we'd patch things up over dinner at one of those great New York restaurants you read about.

Nothing! In my case, water over the dam. However, my friend who is still at the same company with him, is heartbroken in his own way. All this hurt over what? MONEY! Sad but true.

I feel it's important to keep a forward momentum. To move on with your life even when you got "poked" by someone you thought you knew. People change, we never know where someone is on his or her path along their journey! Stay strong with your own journey! Wish those who cause you pain, disappointment or cause for concern, well. Take the lesson with a grateful spirit. A true friend is valuable, but as anything of value, friendship takes work! It's not always easy to find someone, other than your own family, who knows you and can maybe see what you're missing. That someone, who can offer a new light, provide direction, or offer discussion without judgment... is priceless! Friends will come and go; however, true friends are there for life!

I've had friends throughout my life, who I felt certain, would be with me along my entire journey. Sadly, this has not been the case. There have been some who chose a different path. I was hurt at the time and missed our interactions together, yet in the end you have to weigh the options and decide, is this friendship really worth it? I've learned that in life you have to leave yourself open to friendships both new and old. Maybe it's age, or past experiences, but I find myself being more discerning regarding both.

During this worldwide pandemic, I have been flattered and oh, so grateful for the friends, fans, and acquaintances who have reached out to me and my family to see how we are and wish us the best. Unbelievable! It has been a huge help towards alleviating my concerns about income, future jobs, and kids. The support we have received has only made me stronger in my resolve... I've taken the right path!

Jo Anne Worley

Tommy Smothers

Paula Poundstone

Chapter 15

MILLENNIALS

●

MAYBE IF WE TELL THEM THEIR BRAIN IS AN APP, THEY'LL START USING IT.
-Unknown

OK, have I been in a coma and just woke up and the world has changed? This phone business... I walk around New York City screaming out, "Heads up!" Everyone is walking around texting, talking, Instagramming, Tweeting, TikToking, Facebooking. What happened to talking face-to-face? That's how you can see the true emotion from another human being. You can see what they're hiding, what they're not saying, the true genuineness of a person, the true essence of connection between two people.

This cell phone business empowers people but does not do a thing to show who that person is. My daughter yells at me, "Why don't you take your phone with you?" I reply, "Because I'm out to dinner and don't want to be bothered with the phone. I want to speak to a person and enjoy their company and look in their eyes and have a nice conversation." I sit in restaurants and look at tables of people sitting together yet staring at their cell phones. No one is speaking! It's an empty dialogue. I recently watched a couple sit down to eat at a restaurant, order their food, go to their cell phones and not speak to one another the whole sixty-five minutes they were there. My wife would have taken the phone and thrown it down and smashed it on the floor. Is that old school? Maybe, but I like it! A cell phone to us while growing up was a telephone in prison. A prisoner was calling on the phone from his jail cell! Really, what's so important that you can't wait until you see that person to sit and talk? Yes, I can understand something has come up and it's important to communicate immediately. But to me, the content of these phone conversations is tearing us apart as a people and as a country. The weak use it to hide behind, the insecure use it for strength, the lonely use it for company. Whatever you use it for, understand what you're doing and why.

Technology allows us to get information we need at the tip of our fingers. That's amazing, but the downside is, your information is being exploited all over the internet! Your likes, dislikes, your family, your personal information. I type into my computer a question about car rentals and within minutes there are at least seven rental companies popping up on my phone and computer. I inquire about a simple vitamin and I'm inundated with information on that vitamin as well as fifty others. I was sitting in my apartment in New York and did not realize there was one of those speaker gadgets around. I was speaking to someone on the phone, inquiring about a good restaurant close by to eat. Within minutes the gadget starts reeling off the names of six restaurants around my neighborhood. Be careful, Big Brother is listening! They say now that a three-year-old can unlock an iPhone, go to the apps they know and work it. When I was three, I got my tongue stuck to an ice tray screaming, "Ma, ma, ma!" At four, I ate dirt!

What's so important that it can't wait? I see people walking around speaking loudly. I think they're talking to themselves or are mentally challenged, only to find out they have ear buds in their ears and are speaking to someone on the phone. Shut up! People are listening, go somewhere else to discuss your life. Some of us don't care and don't want to know. Hello! I see parents using a cell phone to entertain their young children. Great, but what happens when they grow older? I know parents who have used their cell phone with their children for gaming purposes and now both parents and children spend most of their free time on their phones or a computer. What happened to emotions, feelings, communication, the psychological connections of experiencing life's twists and turns? People, come on! Put it in perspective. There's a whole life out there filled with emotions and feelings. To hide from them is hiding from the true essence of living your life. These kids, nothing shocks them but everything surprises them!

People ask me, "Bobby, are you on Instagram, Twitter or Facebook?" Are you kidding me? I'm in life - I hire a person to communicate in that world. I don't want to be immersed in it. People who are small, who want to appear large, use these platforms. For people who are not popular, it allows them to delude themselves, based on their number of likes and followers. However, don't kid yourself, these are not genuine friendships.

Next up. Dating apps: Tinder, Match, Grinder, Hump Me, Dump Me. People place their bios on them and hope to meet another person with the same interests and likes. Remember meeting someone at a bar or being introduced through a friend or at a club? You'd meet, talk, then decide to date or not. I'm a firm believer that there is someone out there for everyone. I remember I was told, "When you meet that one, you'll know!" I did and yes, I knew! And you always know when you're ready. It doesn't happen by magic; you need to do some work on yourself first. I hear from my daughter and her entitled friends that they can't meet someone special, the "one." That's because they still have some work to do on themselves. Then when that special someone walks in the door, you'll know it right away and be able to handle it. Otherwise, you'll be with someone and it just won't work out. Back to the drawing board of yourself. I can sit with someone and in a few minutes know if this person is someone I want to know or not. You will too. No rush! I'd rather be alone and happy with myself, than with someone and be unhappy. It's your choice.

I was sitting next to a girl on the plane, it was a cold flight and she was wearing ripped jeans. I had an extra flight blanket and asked her if she would like to use it? She smiled and said, "Yes." We got to talking and I asked her what she paid for those ripped jeans? She replied, "Three hundred and fifty dollars!" I spit my pretzels out! I'm thinking, why not go to Target, buy a pair of cheap jeans for twenty dollars, cut some holes in both legs and bingo...STYLE!!

How about these tattoos everyone has now? Some cover their whole faces and neck. Are you kidding me? Why not just wear a mask? Or you see girls with tattoos on their arms or on their chest! Ladies, keep in mind that when you get older, your skin loosens and stretches, so that little bird tattoo will end up looking like a feather duster! I was brought up that you never put a bumper sticker on a Bentley. Hey, it's your life! Whenever I see a person with a whole face tattoo I wonder, what were you thinking! Maybe, they don't like the way they look so much, they decide to change it. I tell the following story on the stage: I was sitting on a plane and a seat was open next to me (when do you ever find a seat open nowadays?) The flight attendants were closing the door and I started to move some of my stuff over onto the empty seat. The attendant opens the door back up enough to allow this kid to enter the plane. As he's making his way down the aisle, you can't help but notice he has metal all over his face. Studs, rings, chains strung to different parts of his face... he looks like he fell into a tackle box! He sits down next to me, that's when I can see he has twelve rings going across his eyebrows. He looks at me. I look at him and I say, "You should put a shower curtain up there!" Do people not have mirrors in their homes anymore? Hey, look, I'm a person who accepts whichever way the wind blows. LGBTQ, I don't bother anyone. I just want to know where I can go to pee.

I see women all over the country pushing carriages and strollers. I look in and see dogs! Are women giving birth to animals now? They'll be pushing their pets, while their kids are shuffling alongside on a leash! I travel all around this great changing country of ours and see how young women think it's fashionable to have a big butt! They're trying to emulate who they see on television, like Nicki Minaj and Kim Kardashian. When I was a kid, those girls were called, "fat asses!" "Hey, there's Susie, nice girl, fat ass. You put that butt on your head, it will look like a sombrero!" I also see what these young guys are trying to pull off as style. They're wearing their pants low, with the crotch hanging down between their legs. Their underwear is in the right place, but the crotch is hanging to the floor. When I was a kid, we called that "poopy pants!" "Hey, look at Harry, he's wearing his father's pants! Hey, Harry, you have poopy pants!" I watched these two guys coming down the aisle on the plane and everyone was leaning over to look at them, as they passed by. Being a wise ass New Yorker, I scream out "Hey, you guys got poopy pants!" One guy asks, "What's that?" I tell him, "It looks like you shit your pants and you can swing it around both directions!"

Another time, I'm standing in a packed subway, and there's a guy so close he's almost standing on my feet. I couldn't help but stare. He has these wheels in his ears! Really, he has little stagecoach wheels in his ears. He looks back at me, with attitude, and asks, "WHAT?" I point out, "You have wheels in your ears." He comes back with, "You like them?" My response, "Sir, you have wheels in your ears!" Up to then I hadn't noticed he's wearing a sports jacket. So, I ask him, "Where are you going?" He replies, "I'm going on a job interview." I respond, "Watch my lips...you're not going to get the job." He says, "Why not?" "You have wheels in your ears!!" He asks, "Should I take them out?" I tell him, "No, then it'll look like you're shrinking!"

How about the different colors that people young and old are dying their hair; red, orange, pink, and a combination of colors! I like it, yet for some of you, I just want to say, "No, it's not working." Do people not like themselves? I see these young women all over New York and California wearing Daisy Duke shorts with the cheeks of their asses hanging out. Hey, I'm still a man, it's sexy and yes, I look, but some I want to tap on the shoulder and say, "Sorry not working. It looks like you're about to lose something. Try some suspenders to hold your ass up!" Are people not talking to one another? Are parents just not speaking to their children anymore? I speak to people and they tell me they are vegan or only eat organic. I hear some say they are lactose intolerant. Some say they are gluten free. Who cares? I grew up poor, we were thankful just to have a meal to eat. Hopefully, without a rat tail hanging out!

I look on television and see there are so many cooking shows. Cook the food, eat it up and move on! I look around and see people getting caught up in trends in our society like the #MeToo movement. Ladies, if a man treats you badly or tries to sexually molest you, kick him in the balls or spray him with pepper spray and run! Get the hell away from people like that! As for the LGBT...UVWXYZ, Larry, Moe, and Curly, remember to treat people the way you'd want to be treated, with honor and respect no matter what sex you are or what clothes you're wearing or what label you fall under. I find it quite freeing. When I was a kid growing up, if a man wanted to be with another a man, he was called a queer, graduating into a faggot, later being more sophisticated and called a homosexual, then gay, leading to the present LGBTQ. Who cares how you choose to lead your life? Be aware there are people in this world who can't contain their ignorance and cannot handle their own sexuality and will take it out on you and me.

In the old neighborhood, whether you were a different color, different sexual orientation, or had special needs, we all took up for that person. We never let anyone belittle someone else, make fun of, pick on, or bully because of who they were or what they wore. We were all in this together and we'd all get through this together. That was the unsaid rule of the street and as far as I am to this day it still is! I am amazed when I watch television and see people around this country of ours so ignorant of how they treat other people!

See people for who they are, listen to people talk, see the direction they're coming from and you'll see new worlds open up. Some agree with your view of life and others have you asking yourself, "What Kool-Aid did you drink? What planet have you been living on?" Put your view out there and learn someone's else's viewpoint. Educate yourself and others!

Every generation has language specific to their time. In the 20's you had, BUTT ME (I'd like a cigarette) DARB (Something wonderful) and HAYBURNER (a gas guzzling car). In the 50's you heard words like, ANKLE-BITER (A small child) CIRCLED (Married) or QUEEN (A popular girl.) The 80's gave us words like, GNARLY (Dangerous) RADICAL (Outrageous) and one of my favorites, BODACIOUS (Wonderful, very enjoyable.) Young people of today use initialisms, LOL (Laugh out loud) OMG (Oh, my God.) SKRT (Rapidly leaving) or TBH (To be honest). I've come up with a couple of (what I like to call geezer ones) ATD (At the doctor) GTPA (Got to pee again) and of course (FWICIH) (Forget why I came in here.) New words are making their way into our vocabularies all the time, ghosting, binge watch and gas lighting, are examples of relatively new ones. I guess what I'd like to say to Millennials is, don't make your life about Instagram, Snapchat, Facebook or anything that limits the time you spend with REAL people, engaging in REAL conversations. Look up once in a while, engage in and embrace life. Actual reality is much more exciting, intimate and fulfilling! Things like YouTube, and TikTok have their place, as a way to entertain yourself, just don't allow technology to become a substitute for human connection.

Melissa Villaseñor

Paul Rudd

Bill Burr

Mario Lopez

Chapter 16

NEW YORK CITY

●

BABY I'M FROM NEW YORK, CONCRETE JUNGLE WHERE DREAMS ARE MADE OF, THERE'S NOTHING YOU CAN'T DO NOW YOU'RE IN NEW YORK...
-Alicia Keys

I've had my apartment in Greenwich Village for over forty years. When I first rented this apartment in a doorman building, it was five hundred dollars a month, for a six hundred square foot studio apartment (which made it a NYC large studio!) However, it had a secret...there was a small, walled in, concrete patio attached to the apartment! At that time, this location was not such a great neighborhood. I loved it! It was close to everything I needed - the New York subway system, Union Square Park to walk through, or hang out at to watch people. There's a grocery store around the corner, a movie theater in the next block, just everything within walking distance.

I love New York, its people, the stores, and my building. You learn a lot from living in a huge building. You get friendly with the doormen, who basically run and know everything about the people living there. I became friendly with some residents in passing and really liked the building setup. You could take the elevator up the twentieth floor and walk up another flight to be on the roof. What a place to look out and see the sights of this great city! From up above you could see different neighborhoods. From the classy areas where the rent's expensive (you can tell by the design of the buildings) to the shitty areas. Those where the drug dealers lived and sold their products. Here you'd find the park where the junkies would hang out, looking for hand-outs, and the ground was littered with needles! I loved walking through all the different neighborhoods, seeing the different types of people. There were the educated who dressed in classic wear, the rich who wore designer label signature outfits alongside the hard-working class who were glad just to be going to and from work! Everyone in my building liked me and it was comforting to come back after working and go into a safe, familiar zone. I'd look at the small mom and pop stores, each bringing their own original merchandise from wherever to New York City. These were the stores that brought variety and a diverse taste of the world. Boy, has that changed! Now there are the same big department stores you see in every city, carrying the same merchandise. I miss the different styles and design you could choose from in the smaller stores, now it's, "Oh, you got that sweater from Bloomingdale's. I saw it in the paper on sale." The society of sameness is prevalent.

After a while, I was outgrowing my small studio apartment. A friend of mine who was living in Brooklyn, a mere twenty-minute subway ride away, was leaving his third-floor walk-up apartment in a brownstone building. A brownstone building consisted of three apartments, one on each floor. Each apartment had two or three bedrooms, a living room, dining room, kitchen, fireplace, huge closet space, and was a walkup (no elevator.) I met the owner landlord from (Yemen) who lived on the first floor with his adorable family. I moved in and was paying $550, and it was all mine! I kept my small studio in the city and rented it out for $600. So, in essence, I was making $50 a month while living just a little further from the city in a huge, homey, classy brownstone apartment in Brooklyn, New York. It was great! I could actually own a car and find parking, unlike most New Yorkers living in Manhattan, who rent a space in Queens for $250 a month. I loved it there. I joined a private, recreational athletic club which cost much less than an equivalent one in Manhattan. I was in the city working so much, living in Brooklyn gave me a breather, a rest from Manhattan; to leave all that behind (even if it was just to sleep!)

My landlord was wonderful, he worked for the city school district as a janitor to cover his family's insurance expenses. He also owned a Middle Eastern restaurant about a block away from the brownstone called Almotassers. It was popular and you could eat enough hummus there to kill a camel! I'd play catch with his daughters out in the street. They were the sweetest kids.

As I've said, my landlord lived on the first floor, Jill and I were on the third floor and in between on the second floor, was a nut job named Carol. I would work all day in the garment center, come back home to Brooklyn and then high tail it back into the city to perform at comedy clubs. I'd get home by eleven-thirty or twelve midnight feeling great, but tired. Many times, even though I made every effort to not make any noise coming into our apartment; Carol, from her apartment below, would bang a broomstick on her ceiling! Which, for those of you who are unfamiliar with the language of apartments, means, "Knock it off!" She was just the type of person who would look for anything, with anyone, to complain

141

about. I was nice to her (kill 'em with kindness) yet you could see this was her peculiar way of social interaction...read nut job! I would apologize kindly to her, while pointing out that I was very quiet when I came home late at night. Once, at the beginning of our dating relationship, I brought Jill over to my apartment. She couldn't believe the size of my apartment! She looked around and asked me, "This is yours and you live here by yourself?" I replied with a cool, arrogant look, Oh, yeah. She responded, "You're an asshole!" We both laughed but she really couldn't believe I lived here by myself! One night, Jill heard a knock at the door. I went to answer it, opened the door to find Carol standing there. She starts complaining about how loud I am and that I have no consideration for anyone else (same old story.) I tell her in a very menacing tone, "Carol, get the hell downstairs, shut your mouth and get a life, otherwise I'm going to throw you down the stairs right now!" And I slammed the door in her face. I smiled to myself as I walked back to Jill. She's looking at me like I'm a crazy man! I could see she was upset when she said, "I can't believe you just spoke to that person like that and threatened to throw her down the stairs!" Still upset with me I tell her, "No, it's not like that! She's the crazy downstairs tenant, a real nut job." Jill is gathering her things up to leave, now with a look on her face that's telegraphing, "I didn't expect to see this guy act like this. What was I missing? I thought he was a funny, kind, endearing, caring man, not one of those crazies you read about all the time in the paper, a psycho!" I went on to further explain that this woman complained all the time. How the landlord, Nasser, was well aware of her caustic interpersonal behavior. He felt sorry for her and that's why he allowed her to stay! He felt badly for her! Fast forward about eight months and Jill has moved in with me and we're having a ball. She's working three waitressing jobs and I'm doing my day job as well as performing every night. Eventually traveling from Tuesday through Sunday to comedy clubs around the country. The time spent together was wonderful, filled with laughter, love and a lot of fun!

One day I'm home, there's a knock at the door, Jill goes to answer it and I can hear her as she opens the door. "Carol! I want you to leave right now and don't ever come and knock on this door again. If you do...I will throw you down the stairs!" Jill comes into where I'm sitting, watching tv and I exclaim, "So now you're going to throw her down the stairs! Oh, my God, maybe I'm with the wrong person, who I thought was loving, caring, fun-loving and smart!" We both laughed and never forgot!

Here's the best! One day Nasser asks me to come over to the restaurant to have a talk. He always believed you discussed things over food! I didn't mind, here comes the hummus! He brings up the subject of Carol. I jump in and tell him, "Nasser, she's crazy! Why haven't you gotten rid of her in all this time?" He informs me, "Women get like this in my country (Yemen) and I have seen it so many times! Therefore, after discussing this with my wife (a wonderful lady) a woman like this needs "the fuck "and we would like you, Bobby, to give her 'the fuck.' "He goes on to tell me that many women in his country don't have anyone in their lives, which is why they get all crazy, nervous and uptight. Once they get "the fuck" everything calms down. I crack up and tell him, "Nasser, I would give her "the fuck" - but only with your dick...or maybe a camel's!" He laughs and tells me he understands. They just figured it was worth a try!

Ahh, New York living!

Don't get me wrong, I've traveled and performed in almost every major city and state in the United States. I've loved Chicago, San Francisco, Miami, North Carolina, Boston, New Jersey. All have history and sites to behold, yet there is only one New York City. It seems to have the combined offerings of every city! I just love it!

New York has an unbelievable energy about it – the hustle and bustle of people coming and going, in and out and through of this great city. Many restaurants, some of the finest in the world, are in Manhattan. The theater district (Broadway) is known throughout the world as the best place to see live theater. When I was young, having the opportunity to go to Broadway to see a show inspired me to become a performer! The tremendous onslaught of people living and working and playing in this city is mind- blowing! The architecture all around the city makes you stop and wonder, when was this built? This island called Manhattan is surrounded by two rivers, the East River and the Hudson River. The many museums telling the story of life. I love it, the clubs, the nightclubs, the discos.

There was a club right around the corner from my apartment on 13th street called the Cat Club. I'd be coming home from doing about five comedy spots at different clubs in the city and I'd stop by and say, "Hi!" to the doormen there. They'd tell me great stories about people coming and going in and out of the club. One night they told me, "Bobby, that Donald Trump character pulled up in a limo, got out and walked to the head of the line and started tipping us with fifties, putting on a show for everyone else to see!" "What a dick," but I told them, "Take the money and run!" Laughing, they told me they did. Then they told me there was one woman watching Trump "show off" who caught his attention; her name was Melania. OMG! Donald Trump met his future wife at the Cat Club, one block from my Manhattan apartment! The doormen would ask me all the time if I wanted to come in the club (knowing full well I was a comic with no money to spend on clubbing!) Once and while though, I would take them up, go in and have fun!

Ahh, the stories never end!

The people of New York are so diverse. You can walk the streets and hear so many different languages. The parade of different cultures to watch and listen to is so amazing! The comradery of the people is also truly incredible! Once I was taking my special needs daughter, Madison, for a run in her jogger. I'm singing and laughing with her, when a taxicab cut right in front of us and almost hit her. I pulled her back in time, and thanked God she was all right. At that moment, three people (complete strangers) started yelling at the driver and kicking his taxicab! My people! From the look on that cabbie's face, I doubt if he will ever drive like that again. The people of New York are great! When you get on a subway in New York (or as I translate for Alabama, "An underground train – not a sandwich!") everyone is there for the right reasons. They are going to work or school. Most people are standing, but if someone is sitting in a seat, when a senior person or a special needs person gets on the train and that person doesn't move to allow them to sit? Oh, boy, just watch! The other people standing, look at that individual and say things like, "Ok, get up and give your seat to that person." Or, "Hey pal, time to stretch your legs to help another human being. Sometimes you'll hear, "Yo, pal, get the fuck up NOW and give your seat to him or her." If they don't move (and I've seen that) a cup of soda will get spilled on them or they get their foot stomped on hard by someone. Finally, they'll move! We're all in this together and we will all help and aid each other. I love New York! The simple pastime of people watching is fascinating. You look at all the faces. You see celebrities, moms, students, politicians, rich, poor, all different nationalities binding together to get through the day! The different stores along the streets, the famous stores you read about, the mom-and-pop stores where you discover things you've never seen before, all for purchase! The kindness of people is so evident while touring around the city. When you do come across that one asshole, who is behaving like they are above the rest, people will quickly (and loudly) let them know that they are not!

I grew up eating New York pizza. It's wonderful! People today ask me when they come to New York should they try the pizza? I've tried pizza all around this country and nothing beats a New York pie. People ask me, "Have you tried Chicago thick, deep dish pizza? Sure have – it does not compare. I don't know if it's the New York water (the best in the country) or some sort of NYC alchemy, but it is delicious!

Going to the Empire State building on 34th Street and riding the elevator to the top to view this unbelievable city is eye opening. Taking the Staten Island Ferry downtown for a quick water ride from Manhattan to Staten Island is free. You pass the Statue of Liberty as you cross the harbor to Staten Island as you take in a water perspective of Manhattan. Truly a sight to behold! I tell many people about the ferry when visiting New York, to save them money and see New York. We recently took a ferry to Ellis Island with some friends who came to visit. Ellis Island is a historical site that was open from 1892 to 1954 as the busiest immigrant inspection station in our country. It has an immigration museum showing the history of the arrival of so many different immigrants from around the world. It's breathtaking, I was in awe!

Go to Rockefeller Center where the famous Christmas tree is lit up with the ice-skating rink just beneath it. We make an annual Christmas family trip from California to Manhattan. Which would not be complete without going to Radio City Music Hall to see the world famous Rockettes. The Thanksgiving Day Parade down Fifth Avenue is truly a sight to behold. I've seen parades across this great country of ours but never a parade like this one. Nothing compares with it anywhere! The floats, the bands, the dancing, the music, the people from around the world descending on New York City to view this parade! I'm not what you'd call a museum guy, but even I will go to, and appreciate The Met (the Metropolitan Museum of Art.) It happens to be the largest art museum in the United States.

In the center of New York City is an eight-hundred-and-forty-acre park...Central Park. Where people can go to feel the fresh air, people-watch, and experience the majestic gem. There are spaces for field games, statues, and the one hundred plus year old carousel. There's even a boat house to take a ride around the eighteen-acre lake. People watching in the park is fantastic! I live downtown in Greenwich Village, lower Manhattan, and I'm accustomed to going to Washington Square Park where I can absorb the local air of residency around the park as well as that of NYU (New York University.) In this park, the artwork and the music, as well as the famous fountain in the middle make it a notable spot to visit. They call NYC the city that never sleeps; restaurants will run well into the night; a lot of the bars and clubs stay open till four in the morning. I remember going out to work in a club and then attending an after party and not getting home until 7:00 am in the morning! The fashion you see, and the outfits people wear, the different characters you see on the street are unlike any other city. The energy in this city is off the charts!

I was in New York recently and I was watching this one guy (who I know is a nut job.) The tourists were looking at him and all of a sudden, he takes his pants down and starts dancing in his underwear! They were astonished! I was cracking up - watching them watch him! Ahh, New York, never a dull moment. I love it! Don't get me wrong – I've been to many wonderful cities in our country and abroad, each with its own personality but with a fraction of what New York has to offer. I've seen so many kids from around the country and abroad, apply to schools in New York City. Some just come to visit, either way many end up here permanently. They love my city!

The traffic in New York City is horrendous, in large part due to the many bridges and tunnels used to not only get into, but around the city. The George Washington Bridge crosses over the East River to get to New Jersey, the Fifty-Ninth Street Bridge takes you to Queens. The Verrazano Bridge leads to Staten Island, the Holland Tunnel to New Jersey, and the Lincoln Tunnel, also to New Jersey. The Midtown Tunnel on 34th street goes under the Hudson River leading to Queens and eventually Long Island.

I was once driving to a comedy gig in New Jersey, via the Holland Tunnel, which should take about an hour. Because it was snowing, I leave early, in order to give myself an extra thirty minutes to get there. I got about ten blocks from the tunnel and traffic just stopped! I sat in my car waiting (except when I jumped out and ran into a restaurant to pee!) for an additional forty-five minutes. Then I heard on the news that the Mayor of New York has screwed up the crossing of the George Washington Bridge, and all that traffic was being redirected to the Holland Tunnel! After two and a half hours of trying to move to no avail, I called the venue and cancelled the sold-out job and returned home.

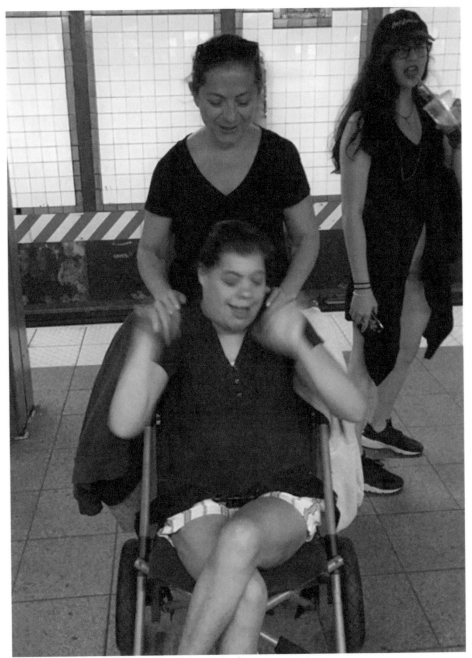

Jill and Maddy 14 th Street subway platform

Typical NYC subway rider

Park Dancer

Bobby and Jill

Chapter 17
PEOPLE

TOO MANY PEOPLE SPEND MONEY THEY HAVEN'T EARNED, TO BUY THINGS THEY DON'T WANT, TO IMPRESS PEOPLE THEY DON'T LIKE.
-Will Smith

I don't find myself being judgmental of people. I look and laugh! I see a person with tattoos all over their body - I just smile and think, Why stop there? Why not put a whole mural across your body and then get someone to pay you to advertise for them? I was brought up to know you never place a bumper sticker on a Bentley. Simply different values. I see the person who has metal all over their face, the ear, the nose, the eyebrows, the chin. It seems to me, it's tough to get a job unless you're a tackle box! There are times when I can't tell the difference between a boy and a girl – LGBTQ. I don't bother anyone; I just want to know where to pee!

I was standing on a corner in New York City, waiting to cross the street and right next to me were these two well-dressed guys, laughing and having fun. All of a sudden, they started kissing each other, full blown making out with tongues going around and around. I was a little uncomfortable for an instant, not my background or my generation. Hey, it's a different world now and that's OK, we're progressing forward, and you have to go with it. When I hear about people hating or demanding that things like marriage, abortion, sex, and gender remain the same based on their upbringing, I say, "Let it go." It's only going to make you crazy and unhappy with the world in front of you. Embrace it and be the example.

Recently I was left alone in our house in Santa Monica, CA, probably for the first time in twenty years. Jill was away cooking three squares a day for eighty-two special needs people, at my daughter Maddy's camp up in Vermont. My other daughter was working and enjoying the summer with her roommates. I was alone with the dog. I loved it! No one was telling me, "Pick up your dirty clothes. Help me make the bed. Bobby, take the garbage out. Walk the dog and take a bag with you this time and no peeing in the neighborhood." I was alone in my castle! Here comes the Fourth of July, on a Wednesday. What to do? I love watching fireworks and a good barbecue, but not this year because of COVID-19.

A friend I've had since high school, Stu, called and invited me to his palatial home south of me in San Juan Capistrano. There will be about eighty people, a band and plenty of food to eat. I'm thinking, I'm in! Until I look up the driving time – two hours and forty-five minutes! Sorry, can't make it. I'm not sitting in traffic for a firecracker! Another couple called and invited me to join them at their friend's house, in Pacific Palisades, fifteen minutes from where I am. They promise great food and a great view of three separate fireworks displays. I hesitate and then agree to go. They pick me up and we go to their friend's house. I, of course, bring a bottle of wine. We went into the house, one of the most beautiful homes I've ever seen. We're greeted by the hosts. The wife, (his fourth) looks as though she has had plastic augmentation from head to toe. If she were to sneeze, her lips would shoot across the room! The husband reminded of a guy who was not very good with the ladies...but makes a lot of money. For the dumb pretty women who are looking for a "fat cat" who would support them, here's your man! Of course, later down the road when they realize he's a butthead, they take the money and run on to the next guy. Oh, he's back out there too, looking for his next hottie, or should I say #DumbLikeaFox5.

I'm standing around, nibbling on something or other. Some people recognize me and ask, "Are you Bobby Collins, the comedian? Can I take a picture with you?" I'm listening to all the jibber jabber going on around me. The conversations all relate to investments, money, real estate, money, trips and how much they cost, cars, homes, money, yachts, private planes, money. I thought my brain was going to explode! Did I just clamp my hand over my mouth? Settle down, you just thought about doing it. However, I did lock my jaw a few times. They were just spewing noise. All these "pretty people" were trying to one-up each other. I wanted to stand in the middle of that room and scream, "You're missing out on LIFE! If your hearts are in the right place, your wallet is full!" They were not people; they were an incarnation of Consumer Reports. I assumed this was what these people wanted to attain in life, to be viewed as successful rich people who display what they have (and there's nothing wrong with that) but come on! When money becomes your god, you're not living, you're existing.

I zoned out and replayed in my head a plane trip I'd taken. I was next to the smelly guy with his feet up on the seat in front of him, the woman talking to me making no sense, I'm thinking, Why don't you roll your head back and forth so I can hear that marble going around and around!

I snapped back when someone says, "Excuse me, do you think the return on art, as an investment, will hold in the long run?" This is success? Come on, you're missing the bigger picture – the love, family, laughter, the excitement, the rewards on the inside, the messages, the spirit, the JOURNEY! I was glad I stayed for those twenty-two minutes. That's all the time it took for me to realize, this is not for me or any of the people I hang around with or would want to know. I politely excused myself and took an Uber home.

I called my wife at my daughter's camp in Vermont and told her the story. She laughed and said she was surprised I stayed that long. I have friends who are billionaires who I hang with and you wouldn't know it at all. One friend owns about four hundred hotels around this country of ours. He is a great guy. He learned everything to start his first motel, from his father. As a result, he and his brothers worked their asses off to learn the business. When my daughter's camp needed some bedding for the cabins, my wife asked my friend, "What do you do with the used sheets from the hotels?" Next thing you know there are two tractor trailer trucks coming up the hill to Zeno Mountain Farm, with eighty new beds and pillows and sheets for the whole camp! Come on people! It's about giving with no expectations of receiving. The rewards come in your heart, seeing special needs people smiling and laughing and enjoying life without placing a money value on things! I love the people I know and the friends I've made over this journey in this life.

I get lectures, every once in a while, from my wife about the people I sometimes work with. She tells me I'm too trusting of people. For someone who can stand in front of thousands of people and know how to work a room when performing, I often cannot see the forest for the trees! I think that everyone is going to have my best interests at hand. Not true! There are people out there who use you for money, fame and anything else they can get their hands on! I've learned. Boy, have I learned. From ambulance chasing lawyers who are trained to steal money, to the agents in the show business ranks who know how to work the system to benefit themselves and not you. There are venue owners who say one thing to get you to work for them and then change their words for the sake of money!

ACKNOWLEGEMENTS

●

For my second time around. No, not marriage. This book. I'd like, again, to thank my girlfriend, my wife, my overseer, my partner - Jill. Boy, it's been some journey! It was thirty-six years ago, we looked at each other and felt that connection. Before that, we both would have run away. Instead, we both knew this was different, this was special...so we ran toward each other. The laughter, the tears, the love, through thick and thin - Thank you! My God! What a journey! Children, homes, travel, friendships, a worldwide pandemic, always climbing the mountain and reaching for the stars! My love, pride and gratitude have no boundaries!

I will always be thankful and grateful to my daughters, for allowing me to join them along their paths. The impact they've had on me! They've taught me - you get what you need, along with the understanding of the why they've been entrusted to you! I've grown along with you, positioned myself in order to relate to you, cherished the time we spend together, and learned something about myself every day. My wish is you always know how much I treasure both of you! OMG did I just say that! My sister once said to me, and I will never forget, "Bobby, I would have never guessed you'd be such a great dad." To see children consigned to me to love, help, teach, and aid. It's been my honor to always want to go that extra mile, for My Girls!

I want to thank the incomparable Sally Lentz, my friend, a comic and a person who can hear my voice whether it's being on a stage or sitting at home typing. It's been a tough year for both of us, but like a true professional you rose up to touch people like only you know how. You can show them a picture of all of us and what we need to hear. I thank you for that!

I want to give a big shout out to my friend Joyce Sherwood, who took the chapters of my book and edited them, as well as to tell me, "Bobby, that does not belong there." My friend for over forty years and a classy lady. Thank you, Joyce.

I'd like to thank my best friends, Colleen and Alan Delman, who through months of a worldwide pandemic we Facetimed every night to see each other and laugh. We would make light of the events in both of our lives and the world for that matter. Boy, did that help!

I'd like to thank Tess, our present dog with whom I've walked every night for a year, I've really gotten to know her personality and character. In my world she probably would have been a stripper, but most definitely a whore. The way she teases the boys in the neighborhood. Yes, those white privileged entitled ones who don't know shit from shinola! She wraps them right around her paws. I'd also like to thank her for knowing not to shit when people are walking by, saving me the task of "properly disposing" of it, after they are gone.

Steve Adler and Susan. Steve, a friend from the old basketball days in New York City, down at the 14th Street Y. Steve, who helped maneuver the publication, copyright, and editing, as well as the book cover and printing. A world I'd never step into. Thank you, Steve. It means a lot. Now pass the ball!

Finally, I would like to thank you, the audience for coming out over the years to see me perform. You've made me a better performer and a better person. I've always appreciate hearing the laughter, the love and the overall camaraderie we share together. The support I've received has made me the father, husband, person I am, and I owe that to you! Thank you.